INTRODUCING
ISSUES WITH
OPPOSING
VIEWPOINTS®

The Next Mass Extinction

M. M. Eboch, *Book Editor*

GREENHAVEN
PUBLISHING

Published in 2018 by Greenhaven Publishing, LLC
353 3rd Avenue, Suite 255, New York, NY 10010

Articles in Greenhaven Publishing anthologies are often edited for length to meet page requirements. In addition, original titles of these works are changed to clearly present the main thesis and to explicitly indicate the author's opinion. Every effort is made to ensure that Greenhaven Publishing accurately reflects the original intent of the authors. Every effort has been made to trace the owners of the copyrighted material.

Library of Congress Cataloging-in-Publication Data

Names: Eboch, M. M., editor.
Title: The next mass extinction / M.M. Eboch, book editor.
Other titles: Introducing issues with opposing viewpoints.
Description: First edition. | New York : Greenhaven Publishing, 2018. |
  Series: Introducing issues with opposing viewpoints | Audience: Grades 9
  to 12. | Includes bibliographical references and index.
Identifiers: LCCN 2017035641 | ISBN 9781534501942 (library bound) | 9781534502789
  (paperback)
Subjects: LCSH: Human ecology--Juvenile literature. | Nature--Effect of human
  beings on--Juvenile literature. | Extinction (Biology)--Juvenile
  literature.
Classification: LCC GF48 .N49 2018 | DDC 304.2--dc23
LC record available at https://lccn.loc.gov/2017035641

Manufactured in the United States of America

Website: http://greenhavenpublishing.com

Contents

Foreword

Indulging in a wide spectrum of ideas, beliefs, and perspectives is a critical cornerstone of democracy. After all, it is often debates over differences of opinion, such as whether to legalize abortion, how to treat prisoners, or when to enact the death penalty, that shape our society and drive it forward. Such diversity of thought is frequently regarded as the hallmark of a healthy and civilized culture. As the Reverend Clifford Schutjer of the First Congregational Church in Mansfield, Ohio, declared in a 2001 sermon, "Surrounding oneself with only like-minded people, restricting what we listen to or read only to what we find agreeable is irresponsible. Refusing to entertain doubts once we make up our minds is a subtle but deadly form of arrogance." With this advice in mind, Introducing Issues with Opposing Viewpoints books aim to open readers' minds to the critically divergent views that comprise our world's most important debates.

Introducing Issues with Opposing Viewpoints simplifies for students the enormous and often overwhelming mass of material now available via print and electronic media. Collected in every volume is an array of opinions that captures the essence of a particular controversy or topic. Introducing Issues with Opposing Viewpoints books embody the spirit of nineteenth-century journalist Charles A. Dana's axiom: "Fight for your opinions, but do not believe that they contain the whole truth, or the only truth." Absorbing such contrasting opinions teaches students to analyze the strength of an argument and compare it to its opposition. From this process readers can inform and strengthen their own opinions, or be exposed to new information that will change their minds. Introducing Issues with Opposing Viewpoints is a mosaic of different voices. The authors are statesmen, pundits, academics, journalists, corporations, and ordinary people who have felt compelled to share their experiences and ideas in a public forum. Their words have been collected from newspapers, journals, books, speeches, interviews, and the Internet, the fastest growing body of opinionated material in the world.

Introducing Issues with Opposing Viewpoints shares many of the well-known features of its critically acclaimed parent series, Opposing

Viewpoints. The articles allow readers to absorb and compare divergent perspectives. Active reading questions preface each viewpoint, requiring the student to approach the material thoughtfully and carefully. Photographs, charts, and graphs supplement each article. A thorough introduction provides readers with crucial background on an issue. An annotated bibliography points the reader toward articles, books, and websites that contain additional information on the topic. An appendix of organizations to contact contains a wide variety of charities, nonprofit organizations, political groups, and private enterprises that each hold a position on the issue at hand. Finally, a comprehensive index allows readers to locate content quickly and efficiently.

Introducing Issues with Opposing Viewpoints is also significantly different from Opposing Viewpoints. As the series title implies, its presentation will help introduce students to the concept of opposing viewpoints and learn to use this material to aid in critical writing and debate. The series' four-color, accessible format makes the books attractive and inviting to readers of all levels. In addition, each viewpoint has been carefully edited to maximize a reader's understanding of the content. Short but thorough viewpoints capture the essence of an argument. A substantial, thought-provoking essay question placed at the end of each viewpoint asks the student to further investigate the issues raised in the viewpoint, compare and contrast two authors' arguments, or consider how one might go about forming an opinion on the topic at hand. Each viewpoint contains sidebars that include at-a-glance information and handy statistics. A Facts About section located in the back of the book further supplies students with relevant facts and figures.

Following in the tradition of the Opposing Viewpoints series, Greenhaven Publishing continues to provide readers with invaluable exposure to the controversial issues that shape our world. As John Stuart Mill once wrote: "The only way in which a human being can make some approach to knowing the whole of a subject is by hearing what can be said about it by persons of every variety of opinion and studying all modes in which it can be looked at by every character of mind. No wise man ever acquired his wisdom in any mode but this." It is to this principle that Introducing Issues with Opposing Viewpoints books are dedicated.

Introduction

"We've never been here as a species and the implications are truly dire and profound for our species and the rest of the living planet."

— climate change expert Guy McPherson

Extinction – when an entire species of living thing dies out – is nothing new. Species have always gone extinct, for a variety of reasons. Some are wiped out by disease. Some lose their habitat due to droughts or floods, ice ages or warming periods. Some are killed when a new species moves in, taking over. Species have even gone extinct through evolving into different species. For all these reasons, most species that have once lived are now extinct.

Usually the world loses about one to five species to extinction every year. This is called the background extinction rate. However, sometimes extinction rates soar dramatically into a "mass extinction." This has happened five times in the distant past, as shown by the fossil record. The most famous mass extinction took place during the Cretaceous period, about 66 million years ago. Some 80 percent of all animal species died out, including the dinosaurs, along with many plant species. Most scientists believe that an asteroid caused clouds of dust that blocked out the Sun, chilling the Earth. When the dust settled, greenhouse gases created by the impact caused the temperature to soar. Few plants and animals could survive these extremes.

Many experts believe we are on the verge of a sixth mass extinction—or that it is already happening. The current extinction rate may be 1,000 to 10,000 times greater than the background rate. We may be losing dozens or even hundreds of species *every day*. By some estimates, the planet will likely lose up to 50 percent of its current species within the next few decades. Furthermore, some scientists believe that human beings may be among the species facing extinction.

Today, human activity is the root cause for many extinctions. Some species are directly killed by humans, such as the dodo and the passenger pigeon, both wiped out through hunting. Whales, sharks, and many other animals on land and in the sea are currently threatened due to fishing or hunting.

Others species die out because of human-created environmental changes. Plants and animals may lose their habitat when forests are cut down or rivers are dammed. Pollution can also cause extinction. For example, toxic runoff from cities and farmland can flow into the ocean, killing fish and coral reefs. Finally, global climate change puts all species at risk. A warming planet changes local habitats, and the plants and animals living there cannot always adapt. Meanwhile, the loss of one species may affect other species. When a single animal or plant dies out, it can have a ripple effect throughout its entire ecosystem.

We know the current extinction rate is unusually high, but it is difficult to determine the exact rate. Many parts of the planet have not yet been explored, so we do not even know how many species currently exist. It is even harder to determine extinction rates of the past. Scientists make estimates based on the fossil record. They can track the number of fossil species found in each past era to determine when those species went extinct. However, only a tiny percentage of living things leave fossils for us to find. It is impossible to say how many species left no record, or left records yet to be found.

The future is even harder to predict. Some scientists have tried, using computer modeling. These models are only as good as the information put into them. Different species react differently to problems such as climate change. Scientists have not yet studied most species in detail, not even many familiar plants and animals that live in our backyards. Groups using different assumptions for their computer models come up with different answers. Without more detailed knowledge of each species, it's hard to know how accurate the models are. Predictions can act as warnings, but we won't know the truth until it happens.

Despite these difficulties, most experts agree that the current extinction rate is dramatically higher than the background rate. They also believe the situation is likely to get worse. In order to stop this trend, people need to take major steps to protect the environment. This includes acting locally to protect vulnerable species. But the most important challenges must be tackled at a global level. Stopping climate change and its devastating effects on the planet will be necessary, according to many scientists.

Most experts working in this field agree that we are currently at risk of another mass extinction. Most also agree that humans are responsible for this devastation. From there, opinions can vary wildly. Many factors cause extinction, and scientists may argue about which are most important. Some people claim that it is too late to stop the next mass extinction, while others say we still have time. Some point out the financial value of protecting the environment or note how specific animals and plants benefit humans. Others claim we have a moral responsibility to protect every species regardless of their benefit to us. Finally, people offer many different plans for tackling the problem. These debates are explored in the viewpoints contained in *Introducing Issues with Opposing Viewpoints: The Next Mass Extinction*, shedding light on this contemporary and controversial issue.

Chapter 1

What Causes Mass Extinction?

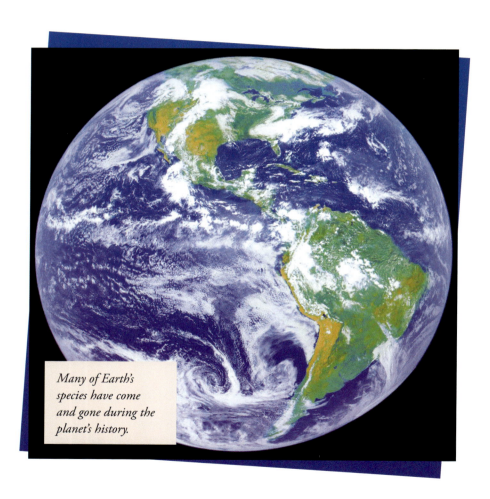

Many of Earth's species have come and gone during the planet's history.

The Dangers of Mass Extinction

Mark Prigg

"Who would have thought that just defaunation would have all these dramatic consequences? But it can be a vicious circle."

In the following viewpoint, Mark Prigg refers to research and scientific papers from international scientists who claim that we are in an era of Anthropocene defaunation. Anthropocene refers to the current age, when humans have a major effect on the environment. Defaunation means the loss of animal species. The scientist quoted believes human activity is causing the extinction of animal species. Large animals have a high risk of extinction, which could alter ecosystems for many species. These imbalances could even affect human health. Meanwhile, the loss of insect species could harm food crops. Prigg is a journalist who specializes in science and technology.

AS YOU READ, CONSIDER THE FOLLOWING QUESTIONS:

1. How many terrestrial vertebrate species have been killed by human behavior, according to the scientific research mentioned?

2. How does the loss of large animal species have a trickle-down effect, according to the article?

3. What effect might an increase in rodents have on human health?

The Earth's six great mass extinction event has already started, scientists have claimed.

They say human behaviour has already killed off over 320 species—and many more are set to follow.

The planet's current biodiversity, the product of 3.5 billion years of evolutionary trial and error, is the highest in the history of life.

But researchers now say it has reached a tipping point.

In a new review of scientific literature and analysis of data published in *Science*, an international team of scientists cautions that while previous extinctions have been driven by natural planetary transformations or catastrophic asteroid strikes, the current die-off can be associated to human activity.

Lead author Rodolfo Dirzo, a professor of biology at Stanford, designates an era of "Anthropocene defaunation."

Since 1500, more than 320 terrestrial vertebrates have become extinct.

Populations of the remaining species show a 25 percent average decline in abundance, and the situation is similarly dire for invertebrate animal life.

Across vertebrates, 16 to 33 percent of all species are estimated to be globally threatened or endangered.

Large animals—described as megafauna and including elephants, rhinoceroses, polar bears and countless other species worldwide—face the highest rate of decline, a trend that matches previous extinction events.

Larger animals tend to have lower population growth rates and produce fewer offspring.

They need larger habitat areas to maintain viable populations.

Their size and meat mass make them easier and more attractive hunting targets for humans.

Although these species represent a relatively low percentage of the animals at risk, their loss would have trickle-down effects that could shake the stability of other species and, in some cases, even human health.

For instance, previous experiments conducted in Kenya have isolated patches of land from megafauna such as zebras, giraffes and elephants, and observed how an ecosystem reacts to the removal of its largest species.

Elephants and other large animals face a high rate of decline.

Rather quickly, these areas become overwhelmed with rodents, grass and shrubs increase and the rate of soil compaction decreases.

Seeds and shelter become more easily available, and the risk of predation drops.

Consequently, the number of rodents doubles—and so does the abundance of the disease-carrying ectoparasites that they harbor.

"Where human density is high, you get high rates of defaunation, high incidence of rodents, and thus high levels of pathogens, which increases the risks of disease transmission," said Dirzo, who is also a senior fellow at the Stanford Woods Institute for the Environment.

"Who would have thought that just defaunation would have all these dramatic consequences? But it can be a vicious circle."

The scientists also detailed a troubling trend in invertebrate defaunation.

Human population has doubled in the past 35 years; in the same period, the number of invertebrate animals—such as beetles, butterflies, spiders and worms—has decreased by 45 percent.

As with larger animals, the loss is driven primarily by loss of habitat and global climate disruption, and could have trickle-up effects in our everyday lives.

For instance, insects pollinate roughly 75 percent of the world's food crops, an estimated 10 percent of the economic value of the world's food supply. Insects also play a critical role in nutrient cycling and decomposing organic materials, which helps ensure ecosystem productivity.

In the United States alone, the value of pest control by native predators is estimated at $4.5 billion annually.

Dirzo said that the solutions are complicated.

Immediately reducing rates of habitat change and overexploitation would help, but these approaches need to be tailored to individual regions and situations.

He said he hopes that raising awareness of the ongoing mass extinction – and not just of large, charismatic species – and its associated consequences will help spur change.

The Five Great Extinction Events

Five times, a vast majority of the world's life has been snuffed out in what have been called mass extinctions, often associated with giant meteor strikes.

End-Ordovician Mass Extinction

The first of the traditional big five extinction events, around 440 million years ago, was probably the second most severe. Virtually all life was in the sea at the time and around 85% of these species vanished.

Late Devonian Mass Extinction

About 375–359 million years ago, major environmental changes caused a drawn-out extinction event that wiped out major fish groups and stopped new coral reefs forming for 100 million years.

End-Permian Mass Extinction (the Great Dying)

The largest extinction event and the one that affected the Earth's ecology most profoundly took place 252 million years ago. As much as 97% of species that leave a fossil record disappeared forever.

End-Triassic Mass Extinction

Dinosaurs first appeared in the Early Triassic, but large amphibians and mammal-like reptiles were the dominant land animals. The rapid mass extinction that occurred 201 million years ago changed that.

End-Cretaceous Mass Extinction

An asteroid slammed down on Earth 66 million years ago, and is often blamed for ending the reign of the dinosaurs.

EVALUATING THE AUTHOR'S ARGUMENTS:

In this viewpoint Mark Prigg reports on a study of scientific literature. He quotes the lead author of the study, a professor of biology. How valuable is expert opinion such as this when it comes to controversial topics? Under what circumstances, if any, should the opinions of scientists hold more weight than the opinions of other people?

Evolution Caused the First Mass Extinction

David Salisbury

"*There is a powerful analogy between the Earth's first mass extinction and what is happening today.*"

The following viewpoint quotes professor Simon Darroch of Vanderbilt University, who claims that evolution caused the world's first known mass extinction. Ediacarans, the first living things made up of multiple cells, arose about 600 million years ago and went extinct after the evolution of animals 60 million years later. The scientist quoted here cites three causes for this extinction: Evolutionary innovation means a species developed a new feature that helped it survive and spread. Ecosystem engineering happens when a living thing creates or modifies its habitat. Biological interactions are the effects that living things have on each other. Salisbury promotes the work of scientists within Vanderbilt University's College of Arts and Science.

AS YOU READ, CONSIDER THE FOLLOWING QUESTIONS:

1. What was the earliest life on Earth, as described in the article?

2. What is the scientific definition of an animal?

3. What does the article mean by the term "ecological engineers"?

"Evidence that Earth's first mass extinction was caused by critters not catastrophe," Vanderbilt University, September 2, 2015. Reprinted by permission.

In the popular mind, mass extinctions are associated with catastrophic events, like giant meteorite impacts and volcanic super-eruptions.

But the world's first known mass extinction, which took place about 540 million years ago, now appears to have had a more subtle cause: evolution itself.

"People have been slow to recognize that biological organisms can also drive mass extinction," said Simon Darroch, assistant professor of earth and environmental sciences at Vanderbilt University. "But our comparative study of several communities of Ediacarans, the world's first multicellular organisms, strongly supports the hypothesis that it was the appearance of complex animals capable of altering their environments, which we define as 'ecosystem engineers,' that resulted in the Ediacaran's disappearance."

Connections to Today

The study is described in the paper "Biotic replacement and mass extinction of the Ediacara biota" published Sept. 2 in the journal *Proceedings of the Royal Society B.*

"There is a powerful analogy between the Earth's first mass extinction and what is happening today," Darroch observed. "The end-Ediacaran extinction shows that the evolution of new behaviors can fundamentally change the entire planet, and we are the most powerful 'ecosystem engineers' ever known."

The earliest life on Earth consisted of microbes—various types of single-celled microorganisms. They ruled the Earth for more than 3 billion years. Then some of these microorganisms discovered how to capture the energy in sunlight. The photosynthetic process that they developed had a toxic byproduct: oxygen. Oxygen was poisonous to most microbes that had evolved in an oxygen-free environment, making it the world's first pollutant.

But for the microorganisms that developed methods for protecting themselves, oxygen served as a powerful new energy source. Among a number of other things, it gave them the added energy they needed to adopt multicellular forms. Thus, the Ediacarans arose about 600 million years ago during a warm period following a long interval of extensive glaciation.

Deckensonia is a fossil from the Ediacaran Period.

"We don't know very much about the Ediacarans because they did not produce shells or skeletons. As a result, almost all we know about them comes from imprints of their shapes preserved in sand or ash," said Darroch.

What scientists do know is that, in their heyday, Ediacarans spread throughout the planet. They were a largely immobile form of marine life shaped like discs and tubes, fronds and quilted mattresses. The majority were extremely passive, remaining attached in one spot for their entire lives. Many fed by absorbing chemicals from the water through their outer membranes, rather than actively gathering nutrients.

Paleontologists have coined the term "Garden of Ediacara" to convey the peace and tranquility that must have prevailed during this period. But there was a lot of churning going on beneath that apparently serene surface.

The Effect of Animals

After 60 million years, evolution gave birth to another major innovation: animals. All animals share the characteristics that they can move spontaneously and independently, at least during some point in their lives, and sustain themselves by eating other organisms or what they produce. Animals burst onto the scene in a frenzy of diversification that paleontologists have labeled the Cambrian explosion, a 25-million-year period when most of the modern animal families— vertebrates, molluscs, arthropods, annelids, sponges and jellyfish— came into being.

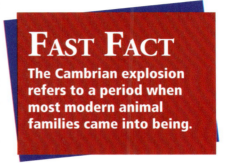

FAST FACT

The Cambrian explosion refers to a period when most modern animal families came into being.

"These new species were 'ecological engineers' who changed the environment in ways that made it more and more difficult for the Ediacarans to survive," said Darroch.

He and his colleagues performed an extensive paleoecological and geochemical analysis of the youngest known Ediacaran community exposed in hillside strata in southern Namibia. The site, called Farm Swartpunt, is dated at 545 million years ago, in the waning one to two million years of the Ediacaran reign.

"We found that the diversity of species at this site was much lower, and there was evidence of greater ecological stress, than at comparable sites that are 10 million to 15 million years older," Darroch reported. Rocks of this age also preserve an increasing diversity of burrows and tracks made by the earliest complex animals, presenting a plausible link between their evolution and extinction of the Ediacarans.

The older sites were Mistaken Point in Newfoundland, dating from 579 to 565 million years ago; Nilpena in South Australia, dating from 555 to 550 million years ago; and the White Sea in Russia, dating also from 555 to 550 million years ago million years ago.

Darroch and his colleagues made extensive efforts to ensure that the differences they recorded were not due to some external factor.

For example, they ruled out the possibility that the Swartpunt site might have been lacking in some vital nutrients by closely comparing the geochemistry of the sites.

It is a basic maxim in paleontology that the more effort that is made in investigating a given site, the greater the diversity of fossils that will be found there. So the researchers used statistical methods to compensate for the variation in the differences in the amount of effort that had been spent studying the different sites.

Having ruled out any extraneous factors, Darroch and his collaborators concluded that "this study provides the first quantitative palaeoecological evidence to suggest that evolutionary innovation, ecosystem engineering and biological interactions may have ultimately caused the first mass extinction of complex life."

EVALUATING THE AUTHOR'S ARGUMENTS:

This viewpoint describes a scientific study that compared sites in Newfoundland, Australia, and Russia. The article explains how the scientists tried to make sure their comparisons were accurate. Does this help support their conclusions? Why or why not?

Viewpoint

3

We Are Causing Mass Extinction

"[A]ll living things – us included – have been plunged into a sickening poisonous stew, with organisms that are unable to adapt pushed further toward extinction."

Paul R. Ehrlich and Anne H. Ehrlich

In the following viewpoint Paul R. Ehrlich and Anne H. Ehrlich argue that human activity is responsible for today's high rate of extinction. As the human population grows, it puts greater stress on the land. More resources are needed to support people. Once people use up the easy resources, they must work harder to access additional resources. This causes even more damage, according to the authors. These factors combine to push other species toward extinction. Paul R. Ehrlich is a Stanford University professor. Anne H. Ehrlich is associate director of the Center for Conservation Biology at Stanford University. Together they are the coauthors of several books on overpopulation and ecology.

AS YOU READ, CONSIDER THE FOLLOWING QUESTIONS:

1. According to the study cited, what percentage of Earth's wildlife has gone extinct in the past 40 years?

2. What do the authors list as the single greatest extinction threat?

3. How are humans competing against other animal species?

"How Humans Cause Mass Extinctions," by Paul R. Ehrlich and Anne H. Ehrlich, Project Syndicate, August 12, 2015. Reprinted by permission. https://www.project-syndicate.org/commentary/mass-extinction-human-cause-by-paul-r--ehrlich-and-anne-h--ehrlich-2015-08.

There is no doubt that Earth is undergoing the sixth mass extinction in its history – the first since the cataclysm that wiped out the dinosaurs some 65 million years ago. According to one recent study, species are going extinct between ten and several thousand times faster than they did during stable periods in the planet's history, and populations within species are vanishing hundreds or thousands of times faster than that. By one estimate, Earth has lost half of its wildlife during the past 40 years. There is also no doubt about the cause: We are it.

We are in the process of killing off our only known companions in the universe, many of them beautiful and all of them intricate and interesting. This is a tragedy, even for those who may not care about the loss of wildlife. The species that are so rapidly disappearing provide human beings with indispensable ecosystem services: regulating the climate, maintaining soil fertility, pollinating crops and defending them from pests, filtering fresh water, and supplying food.

Human Activity

The cause of this great acceleration in the loss of the planet's biodiversity is clear: rapidly expanding human activity, driven by worsening overpopulation and increasing *per capita* consumption. We are destroying habitats to make way for farms, pastures, roads, and cities. Our pollution is disrupting the climate and poisoning the land, water, and air. We are transporting invasive organisms around the globe and overharvesting commercially or nutritionally valuable plants and animals.

The more people there are, the more of Earth's productive resources must be mobilized to support them. More people means more wild land must be put under the plow or converted to urban infrastructure to support sprawling cities like Manila, Chengdu, New Delhi, and San Jose. More people means greater demand for fossil fuels, which means more greenhouse gases flowing into the atmosphere, perhaps the single greatest extinction threat of all. Meanwhile, more of Canada needs to be destroyed to extract low-grade petroleum from oil sands and more of the United States needs to be fracked.

More people also means the production of more computers and more mobile phones, along with more mining operations for the

Oil spills and other harmful human activities are polluting our environment.

rare earths needed to make them. It means more pesticides, deter-gents, antibiotics, glues, lubricants, preservatives, and plastics, many of which contain compounds that mimic mammalian hormones. Indeed, it means more microscopic plastic particles in the biosphere – particles that may be toxic or accumulate toxins on their surfaces. As a result, all living things—us included—have been plunged into a sickening poisonous stew, with organisms that are unable to adapt pushed further toward extinction.

With each new person, the problem gets worse. Since human beings are intelligent, they tend to use the most accessible resources first. They settle the richest, most productive land, drink the nearest, cleanest water, and tap the easiest-to-reach energy sources.

Disproportionate Stress

And so as new people arrive, food is produced on less fertile, more fragile land. Water is transported further or purified. Energy is produced from more marginal sources. In short, each new person joining the global population *disproportionately* adds more stress to the planet and its systems, causing more environmental damage and driving more species to extinction than members of earlier generations.

To see this phenomenon at work, consider the oil industry. When the first well was drilled in Pennsylvania in 1859, it penetrated less than 70 feet into the soil before hitting oil. By comparison, the well drilled by Deepwater Horizon, which famously blew up in the Gulf of Mexico in 2010, began a mile beneath the water's surface and drilled a few miles into the rock before finding oil. This required a huge amount of energy, and when the well blew, it was far harder to contain, causing large-scale, ongoing damage to the biodiversity of the Gulf and the adjacent shorelines, as well as to numerous local economies.

The situation can be summarized simply. The world's expanding human population is in competition with the populations of most other animals (exceptions include rats, cattle, cats, dogs, and cockroaches). Through the expansion of agriculture, we are now appropriating roughly half of the energy from the sun used to produce food for all animals – and our needs are only growing.

With the world's most dominant animal – us – taking half the cake, it is little wonder that the millions of species left fighting over the other half have begun to disappear rapidly. This is not just a moral tragedy; it is an existential threat. Mass extinctions will deprive us of many of the ecosystem services on which our civilization depends. Our population bomb has already claimed its first casualties. They will not be the last.

Greenhouse Gases Contribute to Extinction

Katrin Meissner and Kaitlin Alexander

"Today's rate of change in atmospheric CO_2 is unprecedented in climate archives."

In the following viewpoint Katrin Meissner and Kaitlin Alexander cite evidence that greenhouse gases are rising at an unusual rate. This is a cause for concern because increasing carbon dioxide (CO_2) levels cause higher global temperatures. When ecosystems cannot adapt to these changes, creatures go extinct. The Earth has experienced warming events several times during its history, millions of years in the past. These events ultimately resulted in many species going extinct. The authors believe that this could happen again soon because of currently climbing greenhouse gases. Katrin Meissner is Director of the Climate Change Research Centre at the University of New South Wales in Australia. At the time of this writing, Kaitlin Alexander was a PhD student researching climate change.

1. When CO_2 levels rise, what also rises, according to the article?

2. How do ice sheets provide information on ancient climate conditions?

3. We have records of past warming events. We cannot use these to predict how the Earth will react to current warming, according to the authors. Why not?

We now know that greenhouse gases are rising faster than at any time since the demise of dinosaurs, and possibly even earlier. According to research published in Nature *Geoscience* this week, carbon dioxide (CO_2) is being added to the atmosphere at least ten times faster than during a major warming event about 50 million years ago.

We have emitted almost 600 billion tonnes of carbon since the beginning of the Industrial Revolution, and atmospheric CO_2 concentrations are now increasing at a rate of 3 parts per million (ppm) per year.

With increasing CO_2 levels, temperatures and ocean acidification also rise, and it is an open question how ecosystems are going to cope under such rapid change.

Coral reefs, our canary in the coal mine, suggest that the present rate of climate change is too fast for many species to adapt: the next widespread extinction event might have already started.

In the past, rapid increases in greenhouse gases have been associated with mass extinctions. It is therefore important to understand how unusual the current rate of atmospheric CO_2 increase is with respect to past climate variability.

Into the Ice Ages

There is no doubt that atmospheric CO_2 concentrations and global temperatures have changed in the past.

Ice sheets, for example, are reliable book-keepers of ancient climate and can give us an insight into climate conditions long before

Bleached coral reefs indicate rising sea temperatures.

the thermometer was invented. By drilling holes into ice sheets we can retrieve ice cores and analyse the accumulation of ancient snow, layer upon layer.

These ice cores not only record atmospheric temperatures through time, they also contain frozen bubbles that provide us with small samples of ancient air. Our longest ice core extends more than 800,000 years into the past.

During this time, the Earth oscillated between cold ice ages and warm "interglacials." To move from an ice age to an interglacial, you need to increase CO_2 by roughly 100 ppm. This increase repeatedly melted several kilometre-thick ice sheets that covered the locations of modern cities like Toronto, Boston, Chicago or Montreal.

With increasing CO_2 levels at the end of the last ice age, temperatures increased too. Some ecosystems could not keep up with the rate of change, resulting in several megafaunal extinctions, although human impacts were almost certainly part of the story.

Nevertheless, the rate of change in CO_2 over the past million years was tame when compared to today. The highest recorded rate of change before the Industrial Revolution is less than 0.15 ppm per year, just one-twentieth of what we are experiencing today.

Looking Further Back

To find an analogue for present-day climate change, we therefore have to look further back, to a time when ice sheets were small or did not exist at all. Several abrupt warming events occurred between 56 million and 52 million years ago. These events were characterised by a rapid increase in temperature and ocean acidification.

The most prominent of these events was the Palaeocene Eocene Thermal Maximum (PETM). This event resulted in one of the largest known extinctions of life forms in the deep ocean. Atmospheric temperatures increased by 5–8C within a few thousand years.

Reconstructions of the amount of carbon added to the atmosphere during this event vary between 2000–10,000 billion tonnes of carbon.

The new research, led by Professor Richard Zeebe of the University of Hawaii, analysed ocean sediments to quantify the lag between warming and changes in the carbon cycle during the PETM.

Although climate archives become less certain the further we look back, the authors found that the carbon release must have been below 1.1 billion tonnes of carbon per year. That is about one-tenth of the rate of today's carbon emissions from human activities such as burning fossil fuels.

What Happens When the Brakes Are Off?

Although the PETM resulted in one of the largest known deep sea extinctions, it is a small event when compared to the five major extinctions in the past.

The Permian-Triassic Boundary extinction, nicknamed "The Great Dying", wiped out 90% of marine species and 70% of land vertebrate families 250 million years ago. Like its four brothers, this extinction event happened a very long time ago. Climate archives going that far back lack the resolution needed to reliably reconstruct rates of change.

There is, however, evidence for extensive volcanic activity during

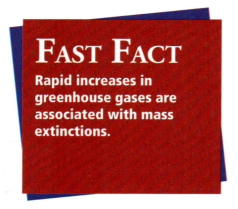

the Great Dying, which would have led to a release of CO_2 as well as the potential release of methane along continental margins. Ocean acidification caused by high atmospheric CO_2 concentrations and acid rain have been put forward as potential killer mechanisms.

Other hypotheses include reduced oxygen in the ocean due to global warming or escape of hydrogen sulfide, which would have caused both direct poisoning and damage to the ozone layer.

These past warming events occurred without human influence. They point to the existence of positive feedbacks within the climate system that have the power to escalate warming dramatically. The thresholds to trigger these feedbacks are hard to predict and their impacts are hard to quantify.

Some examples of feedbacks include the melting of permafrost, the release of methane hydrates from ocean sediments, changes in the ocean carbon cycle, and changes in peatlands and wetlands. All of these processes have the potential to quickly add more greenhouse gases to the atmosphere.

Given that these feedbacks were strong enough in the past to wipe out a considerable proportion of life forms on Earth, there is no reason to believe that they won't be strong enough in the near future, if triggered by sufficiently rapid warming.

Today's rate of change in atmospheric CO_2 is unprecedented in climate archives. It outpaces the carbon release during the most extreme abrupt warming events in the past 66 million years by at least an order of magnitude.

We are therefore unable to rely upon past records to predict if and how our ecosystems will be able to adapt. We know, however, that mass extinctions have occurred in the past and that these extinctions, at least in the case of the PETM, were triggered by much smaller rates of change.

EVALUATING THE AUTHOR'S ARGUMENTS:

In this viewpoint the authors look at past extinctions associated with rising greenhouse gases. They use evidence from the past to predict that we are headed for a mass extinction now. Do they clearly connect evidence from the past to predictions for the future? What are the challenges of predicting the future based on the past?

Viewpoint

5

Our Position in the Galaxy May Be the Clue to Mass Extinctions

"Recognition of this 30-million-year galactic cycle is the key to understanding why extinctions happen on a regular schedule."

Michael Rampino

Most researchers agree that the mass extinction of the dinosaurs 66 million years ago was caused by a massive comet colliding with Earth. In the following viewpoint, Michael Rampino argues that there is physical evidence that similar impacts have occurred every 30 million years. This leads the author to hypothesize that Earth's position in the Milky Way Galaxy is responsible for a cycle in which extinctions and other major geological events, such as volcanic eruptions and big climate changes, result from galactic chaos every 30 million years. Rampino is a Professor of Biology at New York University, focusing on the causes of mass extinctions.

AS YOU READ CONSIDER THE FOLLOWING QUESTIONS:

1. What did the presence of iridium tell scientists?

2. How often do records indicate that mass extinctions and geological impacts occur?

3. What is dark matter?

"How can dark matter cause chaos on Earth every 30 million years?" by Kevin Rey, The Conversation, April 1, 2017, https://theconversation.com/how-can-dark-matter-cause-chaos-on-earth-every-30-million-years-38075. Licensed under CC-BY 4.0 International.

In 1980, Walter Alvarez and his group at the University of California, Berkeley, discovered a thin layer of clay in the geologic record, which contained an unexpected amount of the rare element iridium.

They proposed that the iridium-rich layer was evidence of a massive comet hitting the Earth 66 million years ago, at the time of the extinction of the dinosaurs. The Alvarez group suggested that the global iridium-rich layer formed as fallout from an intense dust cloud caused by the impact. The cloud of dust covered the Earth, producing darkness and cold. In 1990, the large 100-mile diameter crater from the impact was found in Mexico's Yucatan Peninsula.

The timing of this impact, together with the fossil record, have led most researchers to conclude that this collision caused the mass extinction of the dinosaurs and many other forms of life. Subsequent studies found evidence of other mass extinctions in the geologic past, which seem to have happened at the same time as pulses of impacts, determined from the record of impact craters on the Earth. And these co-incidences occurred every 30 million years.

Why do these extinctions and impacts appear to happen within an underlying cycle? The answer may lie in our position in the Milky Way Galaxy.

Our Galaxy is best understood as an enormous disc. Our solar system revolves around the circumference of the disc every 250 million years. But the path is not smooth, it's wavy. The Earth passes through the mid-plane of the disc once every 30 million years.

I believe that the cycle of extinctions and impacts is related to times when the Sun and planets plunge through the crowded disc of our Galaxy. Normally, comets orbit the Sun at the edge of the solar system, very far from the Earth. But when the solar system passes through the crowded disc, the combined gravitational pull of visible stars, interstellar clouds and invisible dark matter disturbs the comets and sends some of them on alternate paths, sometimes crossing the Earth's orbit, where they can collide with the planet.

Recognition of this 30-million-year galactic cycle is the key to understanding why extinctions happen on a regular schedule. But it may also explain other geologic phenomena as well. In further studies,

Scientists believe Earth's interactions with dark matter might drive geologic activity.

we found that a number of geological events, including pulses of volcanic eruptions, mountain building, magnetic field reversals, climate and major changes in sea level show a similar 30 million year cycle. Could this also be related to the way our solar system travels through the Galaxy?

A possible cause of the geological activity may be interactions of the Earth with dark matter in the Galaxy. Dark matter, which has never been seen, is most likely composed of tiny subatomic particles that reveal their presence solely by their gravitational pull.

As the Earth passes through the Galaxy's disc, it will encounter dense clumps of dark matter. The dark matter particles can be captured by the Earth and can build up in the Earth's core. If the dark matter density is great enough, the dark matter particles eventually annihilate one another, which adds a large amount of internal heat to the Earth that can drive global pulses of geologic activity.

Dark matter is concentrated in the narrow disc of the Galaxy, so geologic activity should show the same 30-million-year cycle. Thus, the evidence from the Earth's geo-

logical history supports a picture in which astrophysical phenomena govern the Earth's geological and biological evolution.

And if you're wondering about your own prospects for encountering this dark matter-driven phenomenon? We're just passing through the Galaxy's dense disk within the last couple of million years, so a comet shower may be in the offing.

EVALUATING THE AUTHOR'S ARGUMENTS:

The viewpoint's author, Michael Rampino, presents scientific evidence to discuss the 30-million-year cycle before moving on to propose causes of the cycle. How is this effective? Do you think the author has made a case for why this phenomenon has happened and will happen in the future?

Chapter 2

How Does Mass Extinction Affect People and the Planet?

Melting ice caps are some of the most visible evidence of climate change.

Protecting Nature Saves Money

Anup Shah

"Private and public decisions affecting biodiversity rarely consider benefits beyond the immediate geographical area."

In the following viewpoint Anup Shah discusses the importance of biodiversity. Biodiversity, or a wide variety of living things, helps the planet, according to the author. He also notes many benefits to humans. In fact, one group has tried to estimate the monetary value of genetic resources. Genetic resources are valuable materials from plants, animals, or other natural origins. They may be used to make medicine or other products humans need or want. This viewpoint quotes many statistics showing the value of preserving the environment and biodiversity. In the long-term, protecting nature could save billions of dollars, according to the sources quoted. Shah runs and writes articles for a website called *Global Issues*.

AS YOU READ, CONSIDER THE FOLLOWING QUESTIONS:

1. What is a benefit to having a larger number of plant species, according to the viewpoint?

2. What are some biological resources people use?

3. What percent of world trade is based on biological products or processes, according to the author?

"Why Is Biodiversity Important? Who Cares?" by Anup Shah, Global Issues, January 19, 2014. Reprinted by permission.

An imbalance of the ecosystem can negatively impact biodiversity.

At least 40 percent of the world's economy and 80 per cent of the needs of the poor are derived from biological resources. In addition, the richer the diversity of life, the greater the opportunity for medical discoveries, economic development, and adaptive responses to such new challenges as climate change.
—The Convention about Life on Earth,
Convention on Biodiversity web site

What Is Biodiversity?

The variety of life on Earth, its biological diversity is commonly referred to as biodiversity.

The number of species of plants, animals, and microorganisms, the enormous diversity of genes in these species, the different ecosystems on the planet, such as deserts, rainforests and coral reefs are all part of a biologically diverse Earth.

Appropriate conservation and sustainable development strategies attempt to recognize this as being integral to any approach to preserving biodiversity. Almost all cultures have their roots in our biological diversity in some way or form.

Declining biodiversity is therefore a concern for many reasons.

Why Is Biodiversity Important?

Biodiversity boosts ecosystem productivity where each species, no matter how small, all have an **important role** to play.

For example,

- A larger number of plant species means a greater variety of crops
- Greater species diversity ensures natural sustainability for all life forms
- Healthy ecosystems can better withstand and recover from a variety of disasters.

And so, while we dominate this planet, we still need to preserve the diversity in wildlife.

A Healthy Biodiversity Offers Many Natural Services

A healthy biodiversity provides a number of natural services for everyone:

- Ecosystem services, such as
  - Protection of water resources
  - Soils formation and protection
  - Nutrient storage and recycling
  - Pollution breakdown and absorption
  - Contribution to climate stability
  - Maintenance of ecosystems
  - Recovery from unpredictable events
- Biological resources, such as
  - Food
  - Medicinal resources and pharmaceutical drugs
  - Wood products

- Ornamental plants
- Breeding stocks, population reservoirs
- Future resources
- Future resources
- Social benefits, such as
  - Research, education and monitoring
  - Recreation and tourism
  - Cultural values

That is quite a lot of services we get for free!

The cost of replacing these (if possible) would be extremely expensive. It therefore makes economic and development sense to move towards sustainability.

A report from *Nature* magazine also explains that genetic diversity helps to prevent the chances of extinction in the wild (and claims to have shown proof of this).

To prevent the well known and well documented problems of genetic defects caused by in-breeding, **species need a variety of genes to ensure successful survival**. Without this, the chances of extinction increases.

And as we start destroying, reducing and isolating habitats, the chances for interaction from species with a large gene pool decreases.

[…]

More Important than Human Use or Biological Interest

Many people may support environmental causes to help preserve the "beauty" of Nature. However, that is in a strange way, not really a justifiable excuse as it is a subjective, human or anthropomorphasized view.

For many decades, various environmentalists, biologists and other scientists, have viewed the entire earth as a massive living organism or system due to the interdependent nature of all species within it. Some cultures have recognized this kind of inter-relationship for a very long time. Some have termed this Gaia.

While there are disagreements and differences on how this works, it suggests that ecological balance and biodiversity are crucial for all of earth, not just humans.

Putting an Economic Value on Biodiversity

It was noted earlier that ecosystems provide many services to us, for free.

Although some dislike the thought of trying to put an economic value on biodiversity (some things are just priceless), there have been attempts to do so in order for people to understand the magnitude of the issue: how important the environment is to humanity and what costs and benefits there can be in doing (or not doing) something.

The Economics of Ecosystems and Biodiversity (TEEB) is an organization—backed by the UN and various European governments —attempting to compile, build and make a compelling economics case for the conservation of ecosystems and biodiversity.

In a recent report, *The Economics of Ecosystems and Biodiversity for National and International Policy Makers 2009*, TEEB provided the following example of sectors dependent on genetic resources:

Table: Example of market sectors dependent on genetic resources

Sector	Size of Market	Comment
Pharmaceutical	US$ 640b (2006)	25-50% derived from genetic resources
Biotechnology	US$ 70b (2006) from public companies alone	Many products derived from genetic resources (enzymes, microorganisms)
Agricultural seeds	US$ 30b (2006)	All derived from genetic resources
Personal care, botanical and food & beverage industries	US$ 22b (2006) for herbal supplements US$ 12b (2006) for personal care US$ 31b (2006) for food products	Some products derived from genetic resources. represents 'natural' component of the market.

In addition, it is estimated that implementing REDD (Reducing Emissions from Deforestation and Forest Degradation) could help

- Halve deforestation by 2030, and
- Cut emissions by 1.5 Gt of CO per year.

From a cost perspective (p.18), it is estimated that

- It would *cost* from US$ 17.2 – 33 billion per year
- The estimated benefit in reduced climate change is US$ 3.2 trillion
- The above would be a good return on the initial investment. By contrast, waiting 10 more years could reduce the net benefit of halving deforestation by US$ 500 billion.

In addition, they cited another study that estimated that 3,000 listed companies around the world were responsible for over $2 trillion in environmental "externalities" (i.e. costs that have to be borne by society from ignored factors, or "social costs"). This is equivalent to 7% of their combined revenues and up to a third of their combined profits.

The *BBC* notes that biodiversity is fundamental to economics. For example,

- The G8 nations, together with 5 major emerging economies —China, India, South Africa, Brazil, Mexico—use almost three-quarters of the Earth's biocapacity
- An estimated 40% of world trade is based on biological products or processes.

Despite these free benefits, it has long been recognized that we tend to ignore or underestimate the value of those services. So much so that economic measures such as GDP often ignores environmental costs.

The economic benefits of protecting the environment are well-understood, even if seemingly rarely practiced:

> Numerous studies also show that investments in protected areas generate a cost-benefit ratio of one to 25 and even one to 100 in some cases, [Pavan Sukhdev, from TEEB] said. Planting and protecting nearly 12,000 hectares of mangroves in Vietnam costs just over a million dollars but

saved annual expenditures on dyke maintenance of well over seven million dollars.

—Stephen Leahy, Environment: Save At Least Half the Planet, or Lose It All, Inter Press Service, November 17, 2009

It has perhaps taken about a decade or so — and a severe enough global financial crisis that has hit the heart of this way of thinking— to change this mentality (in which time, more greenhouse gases have been emitted—inefficiently).

Economists talk of the price signal that is fundamental to capitalism; the ability for prices to indicate when a resource is becoming scarcer. At such a time, markets mobilize automatically to address this by looking for ways to bring down costs. As a result, resources are supposedly infinite. For example, if energy costs go up, businesses will look for a way to minimize such costs for themselves, and it is in such a time that alternatives come about and/or existing resources last longer because they are used more efficiently. "Running out of resources" should therefore be averted.

However, it has long been argued that prices don't truly reflect the full cost of things, so either the signal is incorrect, or comes too late. The price signal also implies the poorest often pay the heaviest costs. For example, commercially over-fishing a region may mean fish from that area becomes harder to catch and more expensive, possibly allowing that ecosystem time to recover (though that is not guaranteed, either). However, while commercial entities can exploit resources elsewhere, local fishermen will go out of business and the poorer will likely go hungry (as also detailed on this site's section on biodiversity). This then has an impact on various local social, political and economic issues.

In addition to that, other related measurements, such as GNP are therefore flawed, and even reward unproductive or inefficient behavior (e.g. "Efficiently" producing unhealthy food—and the unhealthy consumer culture to go with it—may profit the food industry *and* a private health sector that has to deal with it, all of which require more use of resources. More examples are discussed on this site's section on consumption and consumerism).

Our continued inefficient pumping of greenhouse gases into the environment without factoring the enormous cost as the climate already begins to change is perhaps an example where price signals may come too late, or at a time when there is already significant impact to many people. Resources that could be available more indefinitely, become finite because of our inability or unwillingness to change.

> ***Markets fail to capture most ecosystem service values.***
> *Existing price signals only reflect - at best - the share of total value that relates to provisioning services like food, fuel or water and their prices may be distorted. Even these services often bypass markets where carried out as part of community management of shared resources. The values of other ecosystem services are generally not reflected in markets apart from a few exceptions (such as tourism).*
>
> *This is mainly explained by the fact that many ecosystem services are 'public goods' or 'common goods': they are often open access in character and non-rival in their consumption. In addition, their benefits are felt differently by people in different places and over different timescales. Private and public decisions affecting biodiversity rarely consider benefits beyond the immediate geographical area.... They can also overlook local public benefits ... in favor of private benefits ..., even when local livelihoods are at stake, or focus on short-term gains to the detriment of the sustained supply of benefits over time....*
>
> *Benefits that are felt with a long-term horizon (e.g. from climate regulation) are frequently ignored. This **systematic under-valuation of ecosystem services** and failure to capture the values is one of the main causes underlying today's biodiversity crisis. Values that are not overtly part of a financial equation are too often ignored.*
> —*The Economics of Ecosystems and Biodiversity for National and International Policy Makers 2009 , p.10*
> *(Emphasis original)*

In effect, as *TEEB*, and many others before have argued, a key challenge will be adapting our economic systems to integrate sustainability and human well-being as well as other environmental factors to give us truer costs (after all, market systems are supposed to work when there is *full* availability of information).

Think of some of the effects this could have:

- Some industrial meat production, which is very harmful for the environment, may become more expensive.
  - For example, as mentioned in the previous link, if water used by the meat industry in the United States were not subsidized by taxpayers, common hamburger meat would cost $35 a pound.
  - Instead of regulation to change people's habits, markets would automatically reflect these true costs; consumers can then make better informed choices about what to consume, e.g. by reducing their meat consumption or demand more ecologically sustainable alternatives at reasonable cost.
- A reduction in meat production could protect forests or help reduce clearance of forests for cattle ranches, which would have a knock-on benefit for climate change concerns.
  - Appropriate investment in renewable energy could threaten the fossil fuel industry though they are trying to adapt to that (perhaps slowly, and after initial resistance). But at the same time, governments that are able to use renewable sources are less likely to find themselves spending so many resources in geopolitical areas (e.g. politics, military, terrorist response to Western presence in Middle East, etc) to protect or secure access to fossil fuels.
- "Cradle to cradle" type of design—where products are *designed* to be produced and recycled or disposed of more sustainably— could considerably reduce costs for producers and consumers alike, and possibly reduce stress on associated ecosystems.

FAST FACT

Cutting deforestation in half by 2030 could save $3.2 trillion in climate change expenses.

- Land that is used to produce unhealthy or marginally nutritious items (e.g. tobacco, sugar, possibly tea and coffee) could be used for more useful or healthier alternatives, possibly even helping address obesity and other issues. (For example, while factoring in environmental costs could make healthy produce more expensive too, expanding production of healthier foods could help contain costs rises to some extent.)
- etc.

How much would such accounting save? It is hard to know, but there is a lot of waste in the existing system. In the mid-1990s, the Institute for Economic Democracy calculated that as much as half the American economy constituted of wasted labor, wealth and resources.

Naturally, those who benefit from the current system may be hostile to such changes, especially if it may mean they might lose out.

This is a clear case of inter-related issues: the health of the environment is strongly tried to our economic choices (i.e. how we use resources), but addressing core short-comings in our economic systems is a crucial political challenge.

EVALUATING THE AUTHOR'S ARGUMENTS:

In this viewpoint Anup Shah discusses some of the financial benefits to protecting the environment. He notes that some people dislike putting an economic value on biodiversity. Yet, he suggests, understanding the financial costs and benefits might encourage people to protect nature. How does considering money affect the discussion of environmental protection? When might it be helpful or harmful to consider the cost and financial benefit of protecting nature?

Extinction Makes Way for New Species

Chris D. Thomas

"The net result is that many more species are arriving than are dying out."

One of the fears related to mass extinction is the role human activity plays in causing the endangerment and extinction of species. In the following viewpoint, Chris Thomas argues that, while it is true that species are indeed dying off and the world is changing, we should open our eyes to the positive aspects of a changing world. The author points out that those species that manage to survive changes in their environment often migrate to other parts of the world and adapt to their new conditions. Sometimes they evolve into new species. Thomas is Professor of Evolutionary Biology at the University of York in the United Kingdom.

AS YOU READ CONSIDER THE FOLLOWING QUESTIONS:

1. How many years ago did the dinosaurs die out?

2. What is an example of an imported species causing a native's extinction?

3. Approximately when can we expect "Genesis Number Six"?

Animals and plants are seemingly disappearing faster than at any time since the dinosaurs died out, 66 million years ago. The death knell tolls for life on Earth. Rhinos will soon be gone unless we defend them, Mexico's final few Vaquita porpoises are drowning in fishing nets, and in America, Franklin trees survive only in parks and gardens.

Yet the survivors are taking advantage of new opportunities created by humans. Many are spreading into new parts of the world, adapting to new conditions, and even evolving into new species. In some respects, diversity is actually increasing in the human epoch, the Anthropocene. It is these biological gains that I contemplate in a new book, *Inheritors of the Earth: How Nature is Thriving in an Age of Extinction*, in which I argue that it is no longer credible for us to take a loss-only view of the world's biodiversity.

The beneficiaries surround us all. Glancing out of my study window, I see poppies and camomile plants sprouting in the margins of the adjacent barley field. These plants are southern European "weeds" taking advantage of a new human-created habitat. When I visit London, I see pigeons nesting on human-built cliffs (their ancestors nested on sea cliffs) and I listen out for the cries of skyscraper-dwelling peregrine falcons which hunt them.

Climate change has brought tree bumblebees from continental Europe to my Yorkshire garden in recent years. They are joined by an influx of world travellers, moved by humans as ornamental garden plants, pets, crops, and livestock, or simply by accident, before they escaped into the wild. Neither the hares nor the rabbits in my field are "native" to Britain.

Many conservationists and "invasive species biologists" wring their hands at this cavalcade of "aliens". But it is how the biological world works. Throughout the history of the Earth, species have survived by moving to new locations that permit them to flourish—today, escaped yellow-crested cockatoos are thriving in Hong Kong, while continuing to decline in their Indonesian homeland.

Nonetheless, the rate at which we are transporting species is unprecedented, converting previously separate continents and islands into one biological supercontinent. In effect, we are creating New Pangea,

the greatest ecological pile-up in the Earth's long history. A few of the imported species cause others to become extinct—rats have driven some predator-naïve island birds to extinction, for example. Ground-nesting, flightless pigeons and rails that did not recognise the danger were no match for a deadly combination of rodents and human hunters.

But despite being high-profile, these cases are fairly rare. In general, most of the newcomers fit in, with limited impacts on other species. The net result is that many more species are arriving than are dying out—in Britain alone, nearly 2,000 extra species have established populations in the past couple of thousand years.

Extinction and Evolution

The processes of evolution also continue, as animals, plants and microbes adjust to the way humans are altering the world around them. Fish have evolved to breed when they are smaller and younger, increasing the chances that they will escape the fisherman's nets, and butterflies have changed their diets to make used of human-altered habitats.

Entirely new species have even come into existence. The "apple fly" has evolved in North America, thanks to European colonials bringing fruit trees to the New World. And house sparrows mated with Mediterranean "Spanish" sparrows somewhere on an Italian farm. Their descendants represent a brand new species, the Italian sparrow. Life on Earth is no longer the same as it was before humans arrived on the scene.

There is no doubt that the rate at which species are dying out is very high, and we could well be in for a "Big Sixth" mass extinction. This represents a loss of biological diversity. Yet, we also know that the Big Five mass extinctions of the past half billion years ultimately led to increases in diversity. Could this happen again? It seems so, because the current rate at which new animals and plants (such as

The heavily fished tiger shark has been given near-threatened status.

the apple fly, the Italian sparrow and Oxford ragwort) are coming into existence is unusually high—and it may be the highest ever. We are already on the verge of Genesis Number Six—a million or so years from now, the world could end up supporting more species, not fewer, as a consequence of the evolution of Homo sapiens.

The ongoing ecological and evolutionary success stories of the Anthropocene epoch require us to re-evaluate our relationship with the rest of nature. Change is ultimately the means by which species survive and turn into new species. So, perhaps we should not spend quite so much time bemoaning the losses that have already taken place, and trying to recreate some imagined past world. We cannot rewind history. It might be more effective for us to facilitate future biological gains even if, in so doing, we move further away from how the world used to be.

This does not let us off the hook—species are genuinely dying out —but it does mean that we should not regard change per se as negative. We should perhaps think of ourselves as inmates and moulders of a dynamic, changing world, rather than as despoilers of a formerly pristine land.

EVALUATING THE AUTHOR'S ARGUMENTS:

What is different about Chris Thomas's viewpoint, compared to others you have read? How would you describe his perspective on mass extinction? Do you agree with his point of view?

Coral Reefs Are at Risk

Anup Shah

"If, and when, [coral reefs] go, they will take with them about one-third of the world's marine biodiversity."

In the following viewpoint Anup Shah discusses the importance of coral reefs. He addresses the value coral reefs provide to other rain animals. He also lists two different estimates of the monetary value coral reefs provide humans. Yet coral reefs are dying, with 20 percent already destroyed and up to 60 percent at risk. Many factors contribute to the threats against coral reefs. These include direct human pressures, such as fishing, as well as worldwide concern, such as climate change. Environmental groups can protect the reefs in some ways, such as limiting fishing. However, they can do little about rising sea temperatures caused by climate change.

AS YOU READ, CONSIDER THE FOLLOWING QUESTIONS:

1. How do coral reefs benefit the environment, according to the viewpoint?

2. How much money do coral reefs provide to the global economy, according to estimates cited?

3. What, according to the author's is the main way to address coral reef problems?

The future of healthy coral reefs is in jeopardy.

Coral reefs cover an area of over 280,000 km² and support thousands of species in what many describe as the "rainforests of the seas."

Coral reefs benefit the environment and people in numerous ways. For example, they

- Protect shores from the impact of waves and from storms;
- Provide benefits to humans in the form of food and medicine;
- Provide economic benefits to local communities from tourism.

The World Meteorological Organization says that tropical coral reefs yield more than US$ 30 billion annually in global goods and services , such as coastline protection, tourism and food.

The US agency NOAA (the National Oceanic and Atmospheric Administration) puts the economic value even higher and says that coral reefs provide economic services — jobs, food and tourism — estimated to be worth as much as $375 billion each year.

In the past few years, however, global threats to coral reefs have been increasing and in the context of the wider environment, the value of coral reefs may be even greater:

> *Ecologically speaking the value of coral reefs is even greater [than these estimates] because they are integral to the well being of the oceans as we know them. ... picture [reefs] as the undersea equivalent of rainforest trees. Tropical waters are naturally low in nutrients because the warm water limits nutrients essential for life from welling up from the deep, which is why they are sometimes called a "marine desert". Through the photosynthesis carried out by their algae, coral serve as a vital input of food into the tropical/sub-tropical marine food-chain, and assist in recycling the nutrients too. The reefs provide home and shelter to over 25% of fish in the ocean and up to two million marine species. They are also a nursery for the juvenile forms of many marine creatures.*
>
> *I could go on, but the similarity with the rainforest should now be clear. Eliminate the undersea "trees", which mass coral bleaching is in the process of doing, and you'll eliminate everything that depends on it for survival.*
> —Rob Painting, Coral: life's a bleach… and then you die,
> Skeptical Science, January 13, 2011

Coral Reefs Are Dying Around the World

IUCN, the International Union for Conservation of Nature, is the world's oldest environmental organization, working around the world.

Periodically, they produce the IUCN Red List of Threatened Species to highlight species that are extinct or extinct in the wild, critically endangered, endangered or vulnerable. Their spatial data shows the threats that coral reef species face around the world:

Australia's Great Barrier Reef is perhaps the best managed in the world. A 2009 report by the Australian agency in charge of it (discussed further below) fears for the future and that "catastrophic damage to the ecosystem may not be averted."

But concerns about coral reefs have been raised for many years around the world.

The *Status of Coral Reefs Around the World, 2004* notes that:

- *20% of the world's coral reefs have been effectively destroyed and show no immediate prospects of recovery;*

- *Approximately 40% of the 16% of the world's reefs that were seriously damaged in 1998 are either recovering well or have recovered;*

- *The report predicts that 24% of the world's reefs are under imminent risk of collapse through human pressures; and a further 26% are under a longer term threat of collapse;*

—Clive Wilkinson,
Status of Coral Reefs of the World: 2004 [PDF format],
World Wildlife Fund, p.7

A report from the World Resources Institute (WRI) in 1998 suggested that as much as 60 percent of the earth's coral reefs are threatened by human activity.

Scientists have said that as much as 95 percent of Jamaica's reefs are dying or dead.

Global Threats to Coral Reefs

All around the world, much of the world's marine biodiversity face threats from activities and events such as

- Coastal development
- Overfishing
- Inland pollution
- Global climate change
- Ocean acidification caused by some of the excess carbon dioxide emissions being absorbed by the world's oceans

The 2004 edition of *Status of Coral Reefs Around the World* lists the following top 10 emerging threats (p.19) in these three categories:

Top 10 Emerging Threats to Coral Reefs

Global Change Threats	Coral bleaching—caused by elevated sea surface temperatures due to global climate change
	Rising levels of CO_2
	Diseases, Plagues and Invasives—linked to human disturbances in the environment
Direct Human Pressures	Over-fishing (and global market pressures)—including the use of damaging practices (bomb and cyanide fishing)
	Sediments—from poor land use, deforestation, and dredging
	Nutrients and Chemical pollution
	Development of coastal areas—for urban, industrial, transport and tourism developments, including reclamation and mining of coral reef rock and sand beyond sustainable limits
The Human Dimension: Governance, Awareness and Political Will	Rising poverty, increasing populations, alienation from the land
	Poor capacity for management and lack of resources
	Lack of Political Will, and Oceans Governance

Climate Change Causing Global Mass Coral Bleaching

The above-mentioned *Status of Coral Reefs Around the World, 2004* also notes (p. 21) that "The major emerging threat to coral reefs in the last decade has been coral bleaching and mortality associated with global climate change."

As explained by Rob Painting on the popular *Skeptical Science* blog, bleaching can occur for a number of reasons such as

- Ocean acidification
- Pollution
- Excess nutrients from run-off
- High UV radiation levels
- Exposure at extremely low tides
- Cooling or warming of the waters in which the coral reside

Bleaching is not new. Past bleaching has often been localized and mild, allowing coral time to recover. But as Painting also adds, *mass coral bleaching on the huge scale being observed certainly appears to be, and represents a whole new level of coral reef decline.*

It is believed that almost all species of corals were affected by high sea surface temperatures during 1998 and the El Niño at the time, which resulted in global coral bleaching and mortality.

2002 was then the second worst year for coral bleaching after 1998.

Although there has been bleaching in the past, since 1998 it has become very severe.In 2010 scientists observed huge coral death which struck Southeast Asian and Indian Ocean reefs over a period of a few months following a large bleaching event in the region. Dr Andrew Baird of the ARC Centre of Excellence for Coral Reef Studies and James Cook Universities was quoted as saying, It is certainly the worst coral die-off we have seen since 1998. It may prove to be the worst such event known to science.

Scientists have long been pessimistic about the future, with some reefs expected to vanish by 2020.

Additional scientific research, reported by *Greenpeace* fears climate change will eliminate reefs from many areas:

> *If climate change is not stopped, coral bleaching is set to steadily increase in frequency and intensity all over the world until it occurs annually by 2030—2070.*
>
> *This would devastate coral reefs globally to such an extent that they could be eliminated from most areas of the world by 2100. Current estimates suggest that reefs could take hundreds of years to recover. The loss of these fragile ecosystems would cost billions of dollars in lost revenue from tourism and fishing industries, as well as damage to coastal regions that are currently protected by the coral reefs that line most tropical coastlines.*
>
> *—Climate Change and the World's Coral Reefs, Greenpeace, 1999*

Despite knowing the causes for many years, Australia's The Great Barrier Reef Marine Park Authority has worried that identifying practicable and effective management responses has proven challenging because traditional management approaches do not work. Coral reef managers are unable to directly mitigate or influence the main cause of mass bleaching: above average water temperatures. This makes mass bleaching a uniquely challenging environmental management problem.

Despite knowing about these issues for many years, conditions have worsened.

At the beginning of September, 2009, the Australian agency looking after the Great Barrier Reef released an outlook report warning the Great Barrier Reef is in trouble:

> *Climate change, continued declining water quality from catchment runoff, loss of coastal habitats from coastal development and remaining impacts from fishing and illegal fishing and poaching [are] the priority issues reducing the resilience of the Great Barrier Reef....*
>
> *[Despite being] one of the most healthy coral reef ecosystems ... its condition has declined significantly since European settlement....*
>
> *While ... there are no records of extinctions, some ecologically important species ... have declined significantly.... Disease in corals and pest outbreaks ... appear to be becoming more frequent and more serious.*
>
> *...*
>
> *Given the strong management of the Great Barrier Reef, it is likely that the ecosystem will survive better ... than most reef ecosystems around the world. However ... the overall outlook for the Great Barrier Reef is poor and catastrophic damage to the ecosystem may not be averted. Ultimately, if changes in the world's climate become too severe, no management actions will be able to climate-proof the Great Barrier Reef ecosystem.*
>
> *—Great Barrier Reef Outlook Report 2009, Great Barrier Reef Marine Park Authority, Australia, September 2009, (pp. i, ii)*

But it is not just the Great Barrier Reef at risk. They are all at risk as Charlie Veron, an Australian marine biologist who is widely regarded as the world's foremost expert on coral reefs, says:

The future is horrific. There is no hope of reefs surviving to even mid-century in any form that we now recognize. If, and when, they go, they will take with them about one-third of the world's marine biodiversity. Then there is a domino effect, as reefs fail so will other ecosystems. This is the path of a mass extinction event, when most life, especially tropical marine life, goes extinct.
—Charlie Veron, quoted by David Adam, How global warming sealed the fate of the world's coral reefs, The Guardian, September 2, 2009

A study published in mid-2012 also found that coral reefs face severe challenges even if global warming is restricted to a 2 degrees Celsius rise which many countries are struggling to agree to meet on given the way climate negotiations have been going for the past decade or more.

FAST FACT
Coral reefs support as many as 2 million other marine species by providing shelter.

There are also concerns that some current assumptions may underestimate the future impact of climate change on corals. Malte Meinshausen, co-author of the study warned:

The window of opportunity to preserve the majority of coral reefs, part of the world's natural heritage, is small. We close this window, if we follow another decade of ballooning global greenhouse-gas emissions.
—Most coral reefs are at risk unless climate change is drastically limited, Potsdam Institute for Climatic Impact Research, September 16, 2012

Legacy of Nuclear Tests
In 1995, France started testing it's Nuclear weapons in the Pacific despite huge protests (though other nuclear nations that are often critical of other countries doing nuclear tests, such as Britain, did

not criticize France). It is now emerging that the coral in the French Polynesia regions where many Nuclear tests have been carried out have been harmed, as the French atomic energy commission has admitted. This is raising concern over what else they may have failed to tell the people who have to live through it in that area.

The Political Will to Address this Has Long Been Lacking

It is recognized that the main way to address coral reef problems is to reduce greenhouse gas emissions and tackle climate change.

However, governments have shown they are unwilling to even commit to the watered down targets set by the Kyoto Protocol, so as *The Guardian* says, "The coral community is not holding its breath." And quoting another respected expert on coral reefs:

> *I just don't see the world having the commitment to sort this one out. We need to use the coral reef lesson to wake us up and not let this happen to a hundred other ecosystems.*
> —David Obura, quoted by David Adam, How global warming sealed the fate of the world's coral reefs, The Guardian, September 2, 2009

EVALUATING THE AUTHOR'S ARGUMENTS:

In this viewpoint Anup Shah says problems affecting coral reefs are hard to remedy. What makes protecting coral reefs so difficult? Does the article suggest solutions or simply describe the problem?

Can We Live Without Bees?

Brian Palmer

"The disappearance of honeybees, or even a substantial drop in their population, would make [many] foods scarce."

In the following viewpoint Brian Palmer takes a close look at something many people don't realize: the value of bees. Bee populations have been dying off in large numbers. Some people claim this is catastrophic for humans, because bees pollinate many food crops. Without pollination, many crops would not produce the food people need to survive. The author explores how important bees truly are to food crops. He notes that, while many foods do not require bee pollination, still people could lose many popular foods if bees go extinct. Palmer is a journalist who covers science, medicine, and the environment.

AS YOU READ, CONSIDER THE FOLLOWING QUESTIONS:

1. Why is 18.7 percent the "magic number" in beekeeping, according to the article?

2. How long are people thought to have been practicing beekeeping?

3. What are some food plants that heavily rely on bees for pollination?

There was more bad news on the honeybee front last week. A U.S. Department of Agriculture report found that honeybee losses in managed colonies—the kind that beekeepers rent out to farmers—hit 42 percent this year.

"Would a World Without Bees Be a World Without Us?" by Brian Palmer, Natural Resources Defense Council, May 18, 2015. Reprinted by permission from the Natural Resources Defense Council.

The human diet relies on the existence of bees.

That number grabbed most of the headlines, but there was more troublesome data below the fold. The magic number in beekeeping is 18.7 percent. Population losses below that level are sustainable; lose any more, though, and the colony is heading toward zero. A startling two-thirds of beekeepers in the USDA survey reported losses above the threshold, suggesting that the pollination industry is in trouble.

For the first time, the USDA reported more losses in summer than winter. Experts can't explain the reversal—especially since the colony collapse disorder epidemic that peaked several years ago seems to have abated. The summer losses may have a single, unknown cause, or a group of known and intensifying causes, such as pesticides or mites.

Today the White House followed the USDA's report with its long-awaited plan to help maintain and grow the pollinator population, including building pollinator gardens near federal buildings and restoring government-owned lands in ways that support bees. It's a good first step.

FAST FACT

Worldwide, 87 crops are typically pollinated by animals, including bees.

The Impact of Bees

Albert Einstein is sometimes quoted as saying, "If the bee disappears from the surface of the earth, man would have no more than four years to live." It's highly unlikely that Einstein said that. For one thing, there's no evidence of him saying it. For another, the statement is hyperbolic and wrong (and Einstein was rarely wrong). But there is a kernel of truth in the famous misquote.

Bees and humans have been through a lot together. People began keeping bees as early as 20,000 BCE, according to the late and eminent melittologist Eva Crane. (Yes, someone who studies bees is a melittologist.) To put that length of time into perspective, the average global temperature 22,000 years ago was more than 35 degrees Fahrenheit cooler than today, and ice sheets covered large parts of North America. Beekeeping probably predates the dawn of agriculture, which occurred about 12,000 years ago, and likely made farming possible.

How important are bees to farming today? If you ask 10 reporters that question, you'll get 11 answers. Some stories say that bees pollinate more than two-thirds of our most important crops, while others say it's closer to one-third. A spread of that size indicates a lack of authoritative scholarship on the subject. My review of the literature suggests the same.

The most thorough and informative study came back in 2007, when an international team of agricultural scholars reviewed the importance of animal pollinators, including bees, to farming. Their results could encourage both the alarmists and the minimizers in the world of bee observation. The group found that 87 crops worldwide employ animal pollinators, compared to only 28 that can survive without such assistance. Since honeybees are by consensus the most important animal pollinators, those are scary numbers.

No Cause for Panic

Look at the data differently, though, and it's clear why the misattributed Einstein quote is a bit of an exaggeration. Approximately 60 percent of the total volume of food grown worldwide does not require animal pollination. Many staple foods, such as wheat, rice, and corn, are among those 28 crops that require no help from bees. They either self-pollinate or get help from the wind. Those foods make up a tremendous proportion of human calorie intake worldwide.

Even among the 87 crops that use animal pollinators, there are varying degrees of how much the plants need them. Only 13 absolutely require animal pollination, while 30 more are "highly dependent" on it. Production of the remaining crops would likely continue without bees with only slightly lower yields.

So if honeybees did disappear for good, humans would probably not go extinct (at least not solely for that reason). But our diets would still suffer tremendously. The variety of foods available would diminish, and the cost of certain products would surge. The California Almond Board, for example, has been campaigning to save bees for years. Without bees and their ilk, the group says, almonds "simply wouldn't exist." We'd still have coffee without bees, but it would become expensive and rare. The coffee flower is only open for pollination for three or four days. If no insect happens by in that short window, the plant won't be pollinated.

There are plenty of other examples: apples, avocados, onions, and several types of berries rely heavily on bees for pollination. The disappearance of honeybees, or even a substantial drop in their population, would make those foods scarce. Humanity would survive—but our dinners would get a lot less interesting.

Humans Are at Risk of Extinction

Dahr Jamail

"We've never been here as a species and the implications are truly dire and profound for our species and the rest of the living planet."

In the following viewpoint Dahr Jamail suggests we may be in the sixth mass extinction. He claims that a number of scientists now believe human extinction is possible in the near future. One such scientist is climate change expert Guy McPherson, whom he interviews. They discuss self-reinforcing feedback loops. This is a system where small changes are enhanced and become bigger. For example, a slight rise in temperature causes an even higher rise in temperature. McPherson claims that many of these feedback loops are at work today. In his view, they are setting up the planet for a massive extinction. Jamail is a staff reporter at Truthout, an independent news organization, and the author of several books.

AS YOU READ, CONSIDER THE FOLLOWING QUESTIONS:

1. What was the "Great Dying"?

2. How many self-reinforcing positive feedback loops has Guy McPherson identified for human-caused climate disruption?

3. How does melting Arctic ice contribute to further climate change?

"Mass Extinction: It's the End of the World as We Know It," by Dahr Jamail, Truthout, July 6, 2015. Reprinted by permission.

uy McPherson is a professor emeritus of evolutionary biology, natural resources and ecology at the University of Arizona, and has been a climate change expert for 30 years. He has also become a controversial figure, due to the fact that he does not shy away from talking about the possibility of near-term human extinction.

While McPherson's perspective might sound like the stuff of science fiction, there is historical precedent for his predictions. Fifty-five million years ago, a 5-degree Celsius rise in average global temperatures seems to have occurred in just 13 years, according to a study published in the October 2013 issue of the Proceedings of the National Academy of Sciences. A report in the August 2013 issue of Science revealed that in the near term, earth's climate will change 10 times faster than during any other moment in the last 65 million years.

Prior to that, the Permian mass extinction that occurred 250 million years ago, also known as the "Great Dying," was triggered by a massive lava flow in an area of Siberia that led to an increase in global temperatures of 6 degrees Celsius. That, in turn, caused the melting of frozen methane deposits under the seas. Released into the atmosphere, those gases caused temperatures to skyrocket further. All of this occurred over a period of approximately 80,000 years. The change in climate is thought to be the key to what caused the extinction of most species on the planet. In that extinction episode, it is estimated that 95 percent of all species were wiped out.

Today's current scientific and observable evidence strongly suggests we are in the midst of the same process - only this time it is anthropogenic, and happening exponentially faster than even the Permian mass extinction did.

In fact, a recently published study in Science Advances states, unequivocally, that the planet has officially entered its sixth mass extinction event. The study shows that species are already being killed off at rates much faster than they were during the other five extinction events, and warns ominously that humans could very likely be among the first wave of species to go extinct.

So if some feel that McPherson's thinking is extreme, when the myriad scientific reports he cites to back his claims are looked at squarely and the dots are connected, the perceived extremism begins to dissolve into a possible, or even likely, reality.

The idea of possible human extinction, coming not just from McPherson but a growing number of scientists (as well as the afore-mentioned recently published report in Science), is now beginning to occasionally find its way into mainstream consciousness.

"A Child Born Today May Live to See Humanity's End, Unless ..." reads a recent blog post title from Reuters. It reads:

> Humans will be extinct in 100 years because the planet will be uninhabitable, according to Australian microbiologist Frank Fenner, one of the leaders of the effort to eradicate smallpox in the 1970s. He blames overcrowding, denuded resources and climate change. Fenner's prediction is not a sure bet, but he is correct that there is no way emissions reductions will be enough to save us from our trend toward doom. And there doesn't seem to be any big global rush to reduce emissions, anyway.

McPherson, who maintains the blog "Nature Bats Last," told *Truthout*, "We've never been here as a species and the implications are truly dire and profound for our species and the rest of the living planet."

Truthout first interviewed McPherson in early 2014, at which time he had identified 24 self-reinforcing positive feedback loops triggered by human-caused climate disruption. Today that number has grown to more than 50, and continues to increase.

A self-reinforcing positive feedback loop is akin to a "vicious circle": It accelerates the impacts of anthropogenic climate disruption (ACD). An example would be methane releases in the Arctic. Massive amounts of methane are currently locked in the permafrost, which is now melting rapidly. As the permafrost melts, methane—a greenhouse gas 100 times more potent than carbon dioxide on a short timescale—is released into the atmosphere, warming it further, which in turn causes more permafrost to melt, and so on.

As soon as this summer, we are likely to begin seeing periods of an ice-free Arctic. (Those periods will arrive by the summer of 2016 at the latest, according to a Naval Postgraduate School report.)

Will there come a day when humans become extinct?

Once the summer ice begins melting away completely, even for short periods, methane releases will worsen dramatically.

Is it possible that, on top of the vast quantities of carbon dioxide from fossil fuels that continue to enter the atmosphere in record amounts yearly, an increased release of methane could signal the beginning of the sort of process that led to the Great Dying?

McPherson, like the scientists involved in the recent study that confirms the arrival of the sixth great extinction, fears that the situation is already so serious and so many self-reinforcing feedback loops are already in play that we are well along in the process of causing our own extinction.

Furthermore, McPherson remains convinced that it could happen far more quickly than generally believed possible—in the course of just the next few decades, or even sooner.

Truthout caught up with McPherson in Washington State, where he was recently on a lecture tour, sharing his dire analysis of how far along we already are regarding ACD.

Dahr Jamail: How many positive feedback loops have you identified up until now, and what does this ever-increasing number of them indicate?

Guy McPherson: I can't quite wrap my mind around the ever-increasing number of self-reinforcing feedback loops. A long time ago, when there were about 20 of them, I believed evidence would accumulate in support of existing loops, but we couldn't possibly identify any more. Ditto for when we hit 30. And 40. There are more than 50 now, and the hits keep coming. And the evidence for existing feedback loops continues to grow.

In addition to these positive feedback loops "feeding" within themselves, they also interact among each other. Methane released from the Arctic Ocean is exacerbated and contributes to reduced albedo [reflectivity of solar radiation by the ice] as the Arctic ice declines. Tack on the methane released from permafrost and it's obvious we're facing a shaky future for humanity.

You talk often about how when major industrial economic systems collapse, this will actually cause a temperature spike. Please explain, in layperson's terms, how this occurs.

Industrial activity continually adds reflective particles into earth's atmosphere. Particularly well known are sulfates produced by burning coal ("clean coal" has a lower concentration of sulfates than "dirty coal"). These particles reflect incoming sunlight, thus artificially cooling the planet.

These reflective particles constantly fall out of the atmosphere, but industrial activity continuously adds them, too. When industrial activity ceases, all the particles will fall out within a few days. As a result, earth will lose its "umbrella" and rapid warming of the planet will ensue. According to a 2011 paper by James Hansen and colleagues, the warming will add 1.2 plus or minus 0.2 degrees Celsius. Subsequent research indicates the conservative nature of this paper, suggesting termination of industrial activity will add a minimum of 1.4 degrees Celsius to the global average temperature.

What indicators are you seeing that show the possibility of major economic collapses in the near future?

We cannot sustain the unsustainable forever, and this version of civilization is the least sustainable of them all. It teeters on the brink, and many conservative voices have predicted economic collapse this year or next. According to a June 2012 report by David Korowicz for the Feasta group, a disruption of supply will trigger collapse of the world's industrial economy in as little as three weeks.

The supply disruptions to which Korowicz refers include water, food and oil. We can add financial credit to the list. In other words, credit could dry up as it nearly did in late 2008. Or the bond markets could trigger hyperinflation. California could have insufficient water to grow enough food to support much of the US, and not long from now. The list goes on.

Go into detail about what you're seeing as far as indications of abrupt climate change.

When I'm in the midst of a speaking tour, as I am now, I deliver a presentation approximately every day. Lately, I include a [different] indication of abrupt climate change [in] each presentation. In other words, I've been coming across evidence every day.

Recent examples include the June 19, 2015, paper in Science Advances: We are in the midst of the sixth great extinction. According to the abstract, the "sixth mass extinction is already under way." The lead author, in an interview, said, "life would take many millions of years to recover, and our species itself would likely disappear early on."

According to data from *The Cryosphere Today*, Arctic ice extent declined 340,000 square kilometers between June 17 and 18, 2015. Such an event is unprecedented. We could witness an ice-free Arctic by September of this year for the first time in human history.

How much temperature increase, over what period of time?

Depending upon the timing of economic collapse and release of the 50-gigaton burst of methane Natalia Shakhova warns about, earth could warm an additional 3 degrees Celsius within 18 months. The relatively slow rate of planetary warming we're seeing so far exceeds the ability of organisms to adapt by a factor of 10,000, according to a paper in the August 2013 edition of *Ecology Letters*.

We depend upon a living planet for our survival. We're killing non-human species at an astonishing rate. To believe we're clever enough to avoid extinction is pure hubris.

Is there an historical precedent for this phenomenon?

There is no historical precedent for ongoing planetary warming. We're dumping carbon into the atmosphere at a rate faster than the Great Dying from about 250 million years ago. That time, nearly all life on earth was driven to extinction.

> ## FAST FACT
> **Humans are dumping carbon into the atmosphere at a rate faster than the Great Dying, when nearly all life on Earth was driven to extinction.**

What does this mean for humans?
How do we cope and survive?

Astonishingly, against cosmological odds, you and I get to live. But not forever. And not much longer.

Coping with the reality of abrupt climate change and human extinction is hardly an easy undertaking. The message I've been delivering for several years is a heavy burden. I suggest fully absorbing the message that we get to live! Part of the process of living is death.

In addition to my latest book [*Extinction Dialogs*], co-authored by Carolyn Baker, I've developed other means for dealing with reality. Among these are a book for young adults co-authored by Pauline Schneider and a workshop co-developed and facilitated by Ms. Schneider. We signed a contract for the book in mid-June and the workshop is described at onlyloveremains.org.

What are some events of late you can point to as evidence that we are already experiencing abrupt climate change?

In addition to the information presented above, there's the ongoing collapse of the Larsen ice shelves in Antarctica, abundant evidence we're headed for a warmer year than 2014 (the hottest year in history), and numerous extreme weather events. These ongoing phenomena have been anticipated for years.

And now, they're here.

What are other factors you feel people should be aware of?

We're in serious human-population overshoot. We're driving to extinction at least 150 species each day. Nuclear power plants require grid-tied electricity, cooling water and people getting paychecks. Without all these, they melt down, thus immersing all life on earth in ionizing radiation.

There's more. Much more. But all the evidence points toward our individual deaths and the extinction of our species in the near future.

But most importantly, we get to live now.

EVALUATING THE AUTHOR'S ARGUMENTS:

In this viewpoint climate change expert Guy McPherson suggests we may be on the verge of human extinction. What evidence does he supply to support this claim? Does he make a compelling case or not?

Chapter 3

Can We Prevent the Next Mass Extinction?

There are many things we can do to preserve nature.

Viewpoint

1

The Sixth Mass Extinction Is Now

"[Y]ou can rouse people to put a lot of energy into trying to save a species .... But it's very, very difficult when a species is down to its last representatives to bring it back."

T. J. Raphael

In the following viewpoint T. J. Raphael refers to an alarming report published in *Science Advances*. This is an online journal published by the American Association for the Advancement of Science. Articles in the journal are reviewed by peer scientists. The report claims that the current extinction rate is unusually high. Scientists compared it to the extinction rate of the past by looking at the fossil record. They believe the current rate signals a sixth mass extinction happening right now. Raphael is the digital content editor for *The Takeaway*, a national news program broadcast on Public Radio International.

AS YOU READ, CONSIDER THE FOLLOWING QUESTIONS:

1. Why does the current extinction rate alarm some scientists?

2. Why is it hard to compare the current extinction rate with the past extinction rate shown by the fossil record?

3. How is human activity changing the oceans, according to the scientist quoted?

Since the year 1900, 69 mammal species are believed to have gone extinct, along with about 400 other types of vertebrates, and the rate at which this is taking place is alarming scientists.

"The evidence is incontrovertible that recent extinction rates are unprecedented in human history and highly unusual in Earth's history," the report says. "Our global society has started to destroy species of other organisms at an accelerating rate, initiating a mass extinction episode unparalleled for 65 million years."

The Study's Conclusion

"The broad definition that's usually offered for a mass extinction is an event that wipes out a large portion of the world's biota, across many different groups of organisms and across many parts of the world," says Elizabeth Kolbert, a staff writer for *The New Yorker* and author of "The Sixth Extinction: An Unnatural History."

The researchers behind this paper—a group of scientists from Stanford University, Princeton University, the University of California at Berkeley, the University of Florida at Gainesville, and the National Autonomous University of Mexico—used very "conservative" estimates to reach their conclusions. And Kolbert says there's a good reason for that.

"One of the complexities that we get into in terms of determining how this extinction event matches up with what's happened in the geological past is that we're looking at apples and oranges," she says. "We're looking at fossil records for past events, and in terms of the present, we don't have a fossil record yet. People are trying to figure out ways to compare these two forms of measurement, and what these scientists did is they took very conservative measurements of what's called the background extinction rate."

The background extinction rate is the rate of extinction that would be expected during "normal times," says Kolbert. In this case,

> **FAST FACT**
>
> Since the year 1900, at least 69 mammal species and about 400 other types of vertebrates have gone extinct. In the past, it might have taken between 800 and 10,000 years for that number of species to disappear.

On the verge of extinction, the California condor has been bred in captivity and reintroduced into the wild.

the researchers used a background rate of two mammal extinctions per 10,000 species per 100 years, and then compared that rate with the current rate of mammal and vertebrate extinctions.

"Even using those very conservative numbers, and also using a very conservative estimate of how many vertebrates have gone extinct, they found very, very high extinction rates," says Kolbert.

What to Do?

Scientists say that the number of species that have gone extinct in the last century should have taken between 800 and 10,000 years to disappear. So what's actually behind this mass extinction?

"There are almost too many [causes] to list right now," says Kolbert.

Though species can die off for any number of reasons, habitat destruction, the transplantation of animals to other places, and of course, climate change, are greatly contributing to the extinction rate. Kolbert says that water contamination is also a big concern.

"Ocean acidification, which is sort of the flipside of climate change," threatens species, Kolbert adds. "As we pour carbon dioxide into the air, a lot of it ends up in the oceans, and when CO_2 dissolves in water, it forms an acid, so we're changing the chemistry of the oceans. We're also pouring nitrogen into the oceans, which creates these huge dead zones which are expanding. The list, unfortunately, goes on and on."

Scientists say intense conservation efforts could slow the subsequent loss of ecosystems, but they say "that window of opportunity is rapidly closing."

"There are an increasing number of species where we know the species has dwindled down to the last hundred individuals—just 20 individuals in the case of the American Condor, for example," says Kolbert, before a concerted effort to save the animals restored the population to about 400. "At that point, you can rouse people to put a lot of energy into trying to save a species and it is a very noble pursuit. ... But it's very, very difficult when a species is down to its last representatives to bring it back."

Thousands of Species Are at Risk

Center for Biological Diversity

"What's clear is that many thousands of species are at risk of disappearing forever in the coming decades."

The following viewpoint states that we are in the middle of the sixth mass extinction. Like the previous viewpoint, it cites the current high rate of species going extinct. This viewpoint, however, focuses on the importance of conserving natural communities. It suggests that all habitats should be protected, whether or not they have great biodiversity. It then covers specific categories of species. For each group, statistics cover the number that are threatened with extinction. In some cases the authors suggest why that group is important or what special risks the group faces. The Center for Biological Diversity is a nonprofit organization whose members advocate to protect endangered species.

AS YOU READ, CONSIDER THE FOLLOWING QUESTIONS:

1. What does this viewpoint claim is the cause of the current mass extinction?

2. How many species have gone extinct in the past 500 years, according to the viewpoint?

3. Why are there probably more extinct species that people do not know about?

"The Extinction Crisis," Center for Biological Diversity. Reprinted by permission.

It's frightening but true: Our planet is now in the midst of its sixth mass extinction of plants and animals — the sixth wave of extinctions in the past half-billion years. We're currently experiencing the worst spate of species die-offs since the loss of the dinosaurs 65 million years ago. Although extinction is a natural phenomenon, it occurs at a natural "background" rate of about one to five species per year. Scientists estimate we're now losing species at 1,000 to 10,000 times the background rate, with literally dozens going extinct every day.[1] It could be a scary future indeed, with as many as 30 to 50 percent of all species possibly heading toward extinction by mid-century.[2]

Unlike past mass extinctions, caused by events like asteroid strikes, volcanic eruptions, and natural climate shifts, the current crisis is almost entirely caused by *us*—humans. In fact, 99 percent of currently threatened species are at risk from human activities, primarily those driving habitat loss, introduction of exotic species, and global warming.[3] Because the rate of change in our biosphere is increasing, and because every species' extinction potentially leads to the extinction of others bound to that species in a complex ecological web, numbers of extinctions are likely to snowball in the coming decades as ecosystems unravel.

Species diversity ensures ecosystem resilience, giving ecological communities the scope they need to withstand stress. Thus while conservationists often justifiably focus their efforts on species-rich ecosystems like rainforests and coral reefs—which have a lot to lose —a comprehensive strategy for saving biodiversity must also include habitat types with fewer species, like grasslands, tundra, and polar seas—for which any loss could be irreversibly devastating. And while much concern over extinction focuses on globally lost species, most of biodiversity's benefits take place at a local level, and conserving local populations is the only way to ensure genetic diversity critical for a species' long-term survival.

In the past 500 years, we know of approximately 1,000 species that have gone extinct, from the woodland bison of West Virginia and Arizona's Merriam's elk to the Rocky Mountain grasshopper, passenger pigeon and Puerto Rico's Culebra parrot—but this doesn't account for thousands of species that disappeared before scientists

Botanists at Everglades National Park search for endangered plants.

had a chance to describe them.[4] Nobody really knows how many species are in danger of becoming extinct. Noted conservation scientist David Wilcove estimates that there are 14,000 to 35,000 endangered species in the United States, which is 7 to 18 percent of U.S. flora and fauna. The IUCN has assessed roughly 3 percent of described species and identified 16,928 species worldwide as being threatened with extinction, or roughly 38 percent of those assessed. In its latest four-year endangered species assessment, the IUCN reports that the world won't meet a goal of reversing the extinction trend toward species depletion by 2010.[5]

What's clear is that many thousands of species are at risk of disappearing forever in the coming decades.

Amphibians

No group of animals has a higher rate of endangerment than amphibians. Scientists estimate that a third or more of all the roughly 6,300 known species of amphibians are at risk of extinction.[6] The current amphibian extinction rate may range from 25,039 to 45,474 times the background extinction rate.[7]

Frogs, toads, and salamanders are disappearing because of habitat loss, water and air pollution, climate change, ultraviolet light exposure, introduced exotic species, and disease. Because of their sensitivity to environmental changes, vanishing amphibians should be viewed as the canary in the global coal mine, signaling subtle yet radical ecosystem changes that could ultimately claim many other species, including humans.

Birds

Birds occur in nearly every habitat on the planet and are often the most visible and familiar wildlife to people across the globe. As such, they provide an important bellwether for tracking changes to the biosphere. Declining bird populations across most to all habitats confirm that profound changes are occurring on our planet in response to human activities.

A 2009 report on the state of birds in the United States found that 251 (31 percent) of the 800 species in the country are of conservation concern.[8] Globally, BirdLife International estimates that 12 percent of known 9,865 bird species are now considered threatened, with 192 species, or 2 percent, facing an "extremely high risk" of extinction in the wild—two more species than in 2008. Habitat loss and degradation have caused most of the bird declines, but the impacts of invasive species and capture by collectors play a big role, too.

Fish

Increasing demand for water, the damming of rivers throughout the world, the dumping and accumulation of various pollutants, and invasive species make aquatic ecosystems some of the most threatened on the planet; thus, it's not surprising that there are many fish species that are endangered in both freshwater and marine habitats.

The American Fisheries Society identified 700 species of fresh-water or anadromous fish in North America as being imperiled, amounting to 39 percent of all such fish on the continent.[9] In North American marine waters, at least 82 fish species are imperiled. Across the globe, 1,851 species of fish—21 percent of all fish species eval-uated—were deemed at risk of extinction by the IUCN in 2010, including more than a third of sharks and rays.

Invertebrates

Invertebrates, from butterflies to mollusks to earthworms to cor-als, are vastly diverse—and though no one knows just how many invertebrate species exist, they're estimated to account for about 97 percent of the total species of ani-mals on Earth.[10] Of the 1.3 million known invertebrate species, the IUCN has evaluated about 9,526 species, with about 30 percent of the species evaluated at risk of extinction. Freshwater inverte-brates are severely threatened by water pollution, groundwater with-drawal, and water projects, while a large number of invertebrates of notable scientific significance have become either endangered or extinct due to deforestation, especially because of the rapid destruction of tropical rainforests. In the ocean, reef-building corals are declining at an alarming rate: 2008's first-ever comprehensive global assessment of these animals revealed that a third of reef-building corals are threatened.

FAST FACT

There are 14,000 to 35,000 endangered species in the United States, according to conservation scientist David Wilcove.

Mammals

Perhaps one of the most striking elements of the present extinction crisis is the fact that the majority of our closest relatives—the pri-mates—are severely endangered. About 90 percent of primates—the group that contains monkeys, lemurs, lorids, galagos, tarsiers, and apes (as well as humans)—live in tropical forests, which are fast disappearing. The IUCN estimates that almost 50 percent of the world's primate species are at risk of extinction. Overall, the IUCN estimates that half the globe's 5,491 known mammals are declining in population and a fifth are clearly at risk of disappearing forever with no less than 1,131 mammals across the globe classified as endangered, threatened, or vulnerable. In addition to primates, marine mammals —including several species of whales, dolphins, and porpoises—are among those mammals slipping most quickly toward extinction.

Plants

Through photosynthesis, plants provide the oxygen we breathe and the food we eat and are thus the foundation of most life on Earth. They're also the source of a majority of medicines in use today. Of the more than 300,000 known species of plants, the IUCN has evaluated only 12,914 species, finding that about 68 percent of evaluated plant species are threatened with extinction.

Unlike animals, plants can't readily move as their habitat is destroyed, making them particularly vulnerable to extinction. Indeed, one study found that habitat destruction leads to an "extinction debt," whereby plants that appear dominant will disappear over time because they aren't able to disperse to new habitat patches.[11] Global warming is likely to substantially exacerbate this problem. Already, scientists say, warming temperatures are causing quick and dramatic changes in the range and distribution of plants around the world. With plants making up the backbone of ecosystems and the base of the food chain, that's very bad news for *all* species, which depend on plants for food, shelter, and survival.

Reptiles

Globally, 21 percent of the total evaluated reptiles in the world are deemed endangered or vulnerable to extinction by the IUCN—594 species—while in the United States, 32 reptile species are at risk, about 9 percent of the total. Island reptile species have been dealt the hardest blow, with at least 28 island reptiles having died out since 1600. But scientists say that island-style extinctions are creeping onto the mainlands because human activities fragment continental habitats, creating "virtual islands" as they isolate species from one another, preventing interbreeding and hindering populations' health. The main threats to reptiles are habitat destruction and the invasion of nonnative species, which prey on reptiles and compete with them for habitat and food.

EVALUATING THE AUTHOR'S ARGUMENTS:

Compared to others in this resource, this viewpoint does not quote many experts in the text. Instead it uses footnotes to indicate sources. Does the use of footnotes give the article more credibility? Why or why not?

Endnotes

1. Chivian, E. and A. Bernstein (eds.) 2008. *Sustaining life: How human health depends on biodiversity*. Center for Health and the Global Environment. Oxford University Press, New York.
2. *Ibid.* and Thomas, C. D., A. Cameron, R. E. Green, M. Bakkenes, L. J. Beaumont, Y. C. Collingham, B. F. N. Erasmus, M. Ferreira de Siqueira, A. Grainger, Lee Hannah, L. Hughes, Brian Huntley, A. S. van Jaarsveld, G. F. Midgley, L. Miles, M. A. Ortega-Huerta, A. Townsend Peterson, O. L. Phillips, and S. E. Williams. 2004. Extinction risk from climate change. *Nature* 427: 145–148.
3. Endangered Species. 2009. In *Encyclopædia Britannica*. Available in Encyclopedia Britannica Online at http://www.britannica.com/EBchecked/topic/186738/endangered-species.
4. Chivian and Bernstein 2008, citing IUCN.
5. Wildlife crisis worse than economic crisis. 2009. Press release. http://www.iucn.org/?3460/Wildlife-crisis-worse-than-economic-crisis--IUCN.
6. Wake, D. B. and V. T. Vredenburg. 2008. Are we in the midst of the sixth mass extinction? A view from the world of amphibians. *Proceedings of the National Academy of Sciences of the United States of America* 105: 11466–11473. http://www.pnas.org/content/early/2008/08/08/0801921105.abstract.
7. McCallum, Malcolm L. 2007. Amphibian decline or extinction? Current declines

dwarf background extinction rate. *Journal of Herpetology* 41(3): 483–491. Copyright Society for the Study of Amphibians and Reptiles.

8. http://www.stateofthebirds.org

9. Jelks, H. J., S. J. Walsh, N. M. Burkhead, S. Contreras-Balderas, E. Díaz-Pardo, D. A. Hendrickson, J. Lyons, N. E. Mandrak, F. McCormick, J. S. Nelson, S. P. Platania, B. A. Porter, C. B. Renaud, J. J. Schmitter-Soto, E. B. Taylor, and M. L. Warren, Jr. 2008. Conservation status of imperiled North American freshwater and diaddromous fishes. *Fisheries* 33(8): 372–407.

10. Klappenbach, L. 2007. How many species inhabit our planet? About.com Guide to Animals. http://animals.about.com/b/2007/08/13/how-many-species-on-earth.htm

11. Tilman, D., R. May, C. L. Lehman, M. A. Nowak. 1994. Habitat destruction and the extinction debt. *Nature* 371:65–66.

Viewpoint

3

Human Activity Is Causing Mass Extinction in the Oceans

Anup Shah

"In losing species we lose the productivity and stability of entire ecosystems..."

In the following viewpoint Anup Shah focuses on the extinction of marine life. He discusses some of the specific factors causing extinction and risk of extinction. Overfishing and damage to coral reefs are blamed for the current fragile state of marine species. He cites whale hunting as an example of how killing one species can disrupt an entire ecosystem. When one species' numbers are reduced, it affects many species around them. Shah suggests that it is not too late to save the oceans. However, currently only a tiny percentage of the ocean is protected. Shah writes articles for a website called *Global Issues*.

AS YOU READ, CONSIDER THE FOLLOWING QUESTIONS:

1. What percentage of large fish have disappeared from the world's oceans, according to the author?

2. What percent of the world's oceans are protected now?

3. How is the loss of sharks likely to affect ocean ecosystems?

"Loss of Biodiversity and Extinctions," by Anup Shah, Global Issues, January 19, 2014. Reprinted by permission.

Despite knowing about biodiversity's importance for a long time, human activity has been causing massive extinctions. As the *Environment New Service*, reported back in August 1999 (previous link): "the current extinction rate is now approaching 1,000 times the background rate and may climb to 10,000 times the background rate during the next century, if present trends continue [resulting in] a loss that would easily equal those of past extinctions."

A major report, the Millennium Ecosystem Assessment, released in March 2005 highlighted a substantial and largely irreversible loss in the diversity of life on Earth, with some 10-30% of the mammal, bird and amphibian species threatened with extinction, due to human actions. The World Wide Fund for Nature (WWF) added that Earth is unable to keep up in the struggle to regenerate from the demands we place on it.

[...]

Consider the following observations and conclusions from established experts and institutions summarized by Jaan Suurkula, M.D. and chairman of Physicians and Scientists for Responsible Application of Science and Technology (PSRAST), noting the impact that global warming will have on ecosystems and biodiversity:

> **Industrialized fishing** has contributed importantly to mass extinction due to repeatedly failed attempts at limiting the fishing.
>
> A new global study concludes that **90 percent of all large fishes have disappeared from the world's oceans** in the past half century, the devastating result of industrial fishing. The study, which took 10 years to complete and was published in the international journal Nature, paints a grim picture of the Earth's current populations of such species as sharks, swordfish, tuna and marlin.
>
> ... The loss of predatory fishes is likely to cause multiple complex imbalances in marine ecology.
>
> Another cause for extensive fish extinction is the **destruction of coral reefs**. This is caused by a combination of causes, including warming of oceans, damage from fishing tools and a harmful infection of coral organisms promoted

Industrial fishing practices have contributed to mass extinction.

by ocean pollution. **It will take hundreds of thousands of years to restore what is now being destroyed in a few decades.**

> *—Jaan Suurkula, World-wide cooperation required to prevent global crisis; Part one— the problem, Physicians and Scientists for Responsible Application of Science and Technology, February 6, 2004 [Emphasis is original]*

[…]

Dwindling Fish Stocks

The UN's 3rd Global Biodiversity Outlook report, mentioned earlier, notes that,

> *About 80 percent of the world marine fish stocks for which assessment information is available are fully exploited or overexploited.*

*Fish stocks assessed since 1977 have experienced an 11%
decline in total biomass globally, with considerable regional
variation. The average maximum size of fish caught declined
by 22% since 1959 globally for all assessed communities.
There is also an increasing trend of stock collapses over time,
with 14% of assessed stocks collapsed in 2007.*
*—Secretariat of the Convention on Biological Diversity
(2010), Global Biodiversity Outlook 3, May, 2010, p.48*

IPS reports that fish catches are expected to decline dramatically in the world's tropical regions because of climate change. Furthermore, "in 2006, aquaculture consumed 57 percent of fish meal and 87 percent of fish oil" as industrial fisheries operating in tropical regions have been "scooping up enormous amounts of fish anchovies, herring, mackerel and other small pelagic forage fish to feed to farmed salmon or turn into animal feed or pet food." This has resulted in higher prices for fish, hitting the poorest the most.

As Suurkula mentioned above, mass extinctions of marine life due to industrialized fishing has been a concern for many years. Yet, it rarely makes mainstream headlines. However, a report warning of **marine species loss becoming a threat to the entire global fishing industry** did gain media attention.

A research article in the journal, *Science*, warned commercial fish and seafood species may all crash by 2048.

At the current rate of loss, it is feared the oceans may never recover. Extensive coastal pollution, climate change, over-fishing and the enormously wasteful practice of deep-sea trawling are all contributing to the problem, as *Inter Press Service* (IPS) summarized.

As also explained on this site's biodiversity importance section, ecosystems are incredibly productive and efficient—when there is sufficient biodiversity. Each form of life works together with the surrounding environment to help recycle waste, maintain the ecosystem, and provide services that others—including humans—use and benefit from.

For example, as Steve Palumbi of Stamford University (and one of the authors of the paper) noted, the ocean ecosystems can

- Take sewage and recycle it into nutrients

- Scrub toxins out of the water
- Produce food for many species, including humans
- Turns carbon dioxide into food and oxygen

With massive species loss, the report warns, at *current* rates, in less than 50 years, the ecosystems could reach the point of no return, where they would not be able to regenerate themselves.

Dr. Boris Worm, one of the paper's authors, and a world leader in ocean research, commented that:

> *Whether we looked at tide pools or studies over the entire world's ocean, we saw the same picture emerging. In losing species we lose the productivity and stability of entire ecosystems. I was shocked and disturbed by how consistent these trends are—beyond anything we suspected.*
> —Dr. Boris Worm, Losing species, Dalhousie University,
> November 3, 2006

"Current" is an important word, implying that while things look dire, there are solutions and it is not too late yet. The above report and the *IPS* article noted that protected areas show that biodiversity can be restored quickly. Unfortunately, "less than 1% of the global ocean is effectively protected right now" and "where [recovery has been observed] we see immediate economic benefits," says Dr. Worm. Time is therefore of the essence.

In an update to the above story, 3 years later, 2009, Dr. Worm was a bit more optimistic that some fish stocks can rebound, if managed properly. But it is a tough challenge "since 80 percent of global fisheries are already fully or over-exploited."

An example of overfishing that has a ripple-effect on the whole fish-food chain is shark hunting.

An estimated 100 million sharks are being killed each year according to the journal, *Marine Policy* which published a report in 2013 representing the most accurate assessment to date (although the challenge in obtaining the data was reflected in their estimate range: 63 —270 million, of which 100 million is the median estimate.

Millions are killed from overfishing and trade. Many die accidentally in fishing nets set for tuna and swordfish, while others are caught for their meat or just for their fins.

A demand for shark-fin soup in places like China and Taiwan is decimating shark populations. Shark fin soup is considered a delicacy (not even a necessity) and can be extremely lucrative. So much money can be obtained just from the fin that fishermen hunting sharks will simply catch sharks and cut off their fins while they are alive, tossing the wriggling shark back into the ocean (to die, as it cannot swim without its fin). This saves a lot of room on fishing boats. Some video footage shown on documentaries such as *National Geographic* reveal how barbaric and wasteful this practice is.

Sharks are known as the "apex predator" of the seas. That is because in general sharks are at the top of the food chain. Without sufficient shark numbers the balance they provide to the ecosystem is threatened because nature evolved this balance through many millennia.

As WWF, the global conservation organization notes, "Contrary to popular belief, shark fins have little nutritional value and may even be harmful to your health over the long term as fins have been found to contain high levels of mercury."

The additional concern is that many of the most threatened species are slow to reproduce, so their populations cannot keep up with the rate they are being needlessly killed.

Another effect of overfishing has been the rise in illegal fishing. But even legal, high-tech fishing has caused other social problems. Poor fishermen in Somalia have found themselves without livelihoods as international fishing ships have come into their area destroying their livelihoods. Some of them have then resorted to piracy in desperation. Clearly not all blame should be laid at the international fishing system as it is also individual choice, but the desperation and other geopolitical issues in the region can turn people to do things they normally would not.

[…]

Declining Ocean Biodiversity

In the past century, commercial whaling has decimated numerous whale populations, many of which have struggled to recover.

Commercial whaling in the past was for whale oil. With no reason to use whale oil today, commercial whaling is mainly for food, while there is also some hunting for scientific research purposes.

Large scale commercialized whaling was so destructive that in 1986 a moratorium on whaling was set up by the International Whaling Commission (IWC). As early as the mid-1930s, there were international attempts to recognize the impact of whaling and try and make it more sustainable, resulting in the actual set up of the IWC in 1946. Many commercial whaling nations have been part of this moratorium but have various objections and other pressures to try and resume whaling.

[…]

Some have argued for whale hunting as a way to sustain other marine populations. National Geographic Wild aired a program called, *A Life Among Whales* (broadcast June 14, 2008). It noted how a few decades ago, some fishermen campaigned for killing whales because they were apparently threatening the fish supply. A chain of events eventually came full circle and led to a loss of jobs:

- The massive reduction in the local whale population meant the killer whales in that region (that usually preyed on the younger whales) moved to other animals such as seals
- As seal numbers declined, the killer whales targeted otters
- As otter numbers were decimated, the urchins and other targets of otters flourished
- These decimated the kelp forests where many fish larvae grew in relative protection
- The exposed fish larvae were easy pickings for a variety of sea life
- Fishermen's livelihoods were destroyed.

This may be a vivid example of humans interfering and altering the balance of ecosystems and misunderstanding the importance of biodiversity.

EVALUATING THE AUTHOR'S ARGUMENTS:

In this viewpoint Anup Shah suggests that the oceans are in crisis but may yet be saved. Given the statistics he cites, does it seem likely that people can save the ocean? Why or why not? What would have to happen?

Act Locally to Save Wildlife

Peter Moyle

"To save wildlife requires positive action; it requires changes in life style and changes in our general way of thinking (or not thinking)."

In the following viewpoint, Peter Moyle says that people have the ability and responsibility to save wildlife. He offers suggestions on how to do so. Many suggestions involve considering the environmental effects of our actions. Lawns could be kept in a more natural state, to reduce the use of pesticides. Readers are encouraged to buy less, reuse items, and then recycle. Moyle also addresses the problems with keeping pets. He notes that cats are especially harmful because they hunt birds and other animals. He blames the loss of wild animals in his home of Davis, California, on pet cats allowed to hunt. Moyle, a former college professor, is associate director of the Center for Watershed Sciences, UC Davis.

AS YOU READ, CONSIDER THE FOLLOWING QUESTIONS:

1. What does the author mean by "neatness is the enemy of wildlife"?

2. How can pets such as cats affect local wildlife when allowed outside?

3. How do wild animals such as coyotes help control the outdoor cat population, as described in the viewpoint?

"What you can do to save wildlife," by Peter Moyle, MarineBio, September 2004. Reprinted by permission. For further reading on this subject, see Marchetti, M. P. and P. B. Moyle. 2010. *Protecting Life on Earth: An Introduction to Conservation Science.* Berkeley: University of California Press. 232 pp.

Introduction

We are the dominant creatures on this planet and we can choose to wipe out most of the species just by continuing on our present course of accelerating population growth and accelerating resource use. To save wildlife requires positive action; it requires changes in life style and changes in our general way of thinking (or not thinking). We must heed the maxim "Think Globally, Act Locally" and realize we are bound with all other forms of life in one gigantic ecosystem. The following are a few of my suggestions of things you can do to help wildlife (and eventually, help yourselves).

Using Time

One of the dominant features of our culture is our obsession with "saving time" as though time were something that could be stored in a deep freeze or bank vault. We consume enormous quantities of energy by using "time saving" gadgets from dishwashers to power lawn movers to garbage disposals. We drive powerful automobiles at speeds slightly faster than the law allows to travel to places as quickly as possible. We eat foods in which there is more energy tied up in the packaging than there is in the food itself. All too often the time "saved" is used for trivial amusement: to watch a TV program or play an extra inning of baseball. As individuals, we need to consider the environmental cost of all this collective time saving and act accordingly. Plan long trips for more leisurely driving. Be willing to take the extra time needed to use public transportation or car pools. Make chores into social activities. Take the few extra minutes needed to mow your lawn with a hand mower (and the good, quiet exercise it provides). I am not suggesting a return to living styles of 200 years ago, just some minor adjustments to our present life styles that might reduce such things as air pollution, which is causing atmospheric warming; the demand for dams that destroy streams; and the amount of habitat covered up by garbage.

Living with Blemishes

Neatness is the enemy of wildlife. Much traditional landscaping, for example, is open and neatly trimmed, with little room for birds and other animals, and it often requires heavy use of fertilizers and pesticides. Let the weeds and bushes grow. Plant native trees. Our demand for unblemished fruit and catsup without insect parts forces the heavy use of pesticides and forces farmers to go to great lengths to control birds and other "pests." Blemished or slightly wormy fruit is still edible. My father had the habit of never eating an apple without taking out his pocketknife and cutting it up. This habit was ingrained from being brought up on a farm in the days before the heavy use of pesticides. Adopting simple habits like this can help to save wildlife (and maybe your own health).

A particularly egregious example of the neatness problem is lawns. Somehow, it is correct in our culture to strive towards a perfect lawn that looks more like an outdoor carpet than something alive. The perfect lawn requires heavy doses of pesticides, herbicides, and fertilizers to keep the monoculture of grass going, akin to field of subsidized corn. Then, when the grass is ready to be harvested, we cut it with a noisy gas-guzzling mower and throw the harvest away (often neatly wrapped in a plastic bag), clogging our landfills. Meanwhile the excess fertilizer and pesticides wind up in the landscape, often washed into streams or lakes via storm drains, where they have toxic effects on fish, ducks, and other aquatic life. Part of the solution is to think of your lawn as an ecosystem and strive for diversity: appreciate the variety of flowers and grasses that push their way through the dominant grass; enjoy the insects that crawl in it or fly over it. Despite the warnings of the lawn care industry, it is possible to have a patch of green to sit and play on without dosing it with nasty substances. Another part of the solution is to reduce lawn area as much as possible, replacing the grass with low-demand ornamentals or a vegetable garden.

Reduce, Reuse, Recycle

"Reduce, Reuse, and Recycle" is a slogan that goes well with "Think Globally, Act Locally." I apologize for presenting these over-used slogans, but they do have a great element of truth to them. All three general activities can make your personal contribution to environmental degradation much less.

Reduce the amount of materials and energy you consume by buying fewer prepackaged goods, driving in an efficient manner (slower, no jack-rabbit starts, etc.), sharing magazines and books, minimizing the use of heating and air conditioning, etc.

Reuse items as much as you can. Many "disposable" items are reusable, especially containers. For example, if you make pomegranate wine (as I used to do) you can use old wine bottles year after year (this wine is drunk young). It is also possible to reuse corks, if they are removed from a bottle with an "ah-so" cork remover. Remember to shop using cloth bags or by bringing "used" bags with you to carry your purchases home.

Recycling is one of the easiest ways to reduce your environmental impact, especially in communities like Davis with curbside recycling programs. Start doing it and it soon becomes a habit instead of a chore. Recycling paper, aluminum, and bottles is so easy, in fact, that it is your responsibility to recycle. If your apartment complex or work place does not have bins for recycling, demand that some be installed. If you have a choice, avoid using materials that cannot be recycled.

Recycling is just one of many things you can do in your daily life to improve the planet. Many other suggestions are provided in detail in dozens of accessible books on recycling and wholesome living available in most book stores. Lack of information is no longer an excuse for not taking positive action to reduce your impact on the global ecosystem.

FAST FACT

A pet cat that is allowed to go outside could kill 200–400 birds per year. With millions of cats in the US, this can have a serious effect on bird populations.

Pets

Most people who keep pets tend to think of them as being more human than animal. Because of this, the goods and services provided to pets and pet owners contribute their share to general environmental degradation. Pets also create special problems in relation to wildlife protection.

Believe it or not, cats can be hazards to wildlife.

There are far too many cats in this world and especially there are too many feral cats, too many abandoned pet cats, and too many pet cats that spend too much of their time stalking wild birds. Cats are natural hunters, even cats that are stuffed daily with pelleted cat chow. Although they kill rats and mice, they rarely have much effect on rodent populations. We are just beginning to appreciate, however, the numbers of birds that cats kill each year. For example, the pet cat of a lighthouse keeper on tiny Stephen Island off New Zealand wiped out a species of wren by itself! Recent studies of cat predation have shown that it is not unusual for a pet cat to kill 200–400 birds per year. Most of the birds are native migrants that are not evolved to handle such an artificially high density of predators. Such migrants are already in trouble due to destruction of nesting habitats and wintering habitats, so the cats are an added cause of their decline. Imagine what it must be like for an inexperienced juvenile white crowned sparrow, reared in the mountains, which follows its parents to spend the winter in the gardens of Davis. Suddenly it is trying to survive in an area with an extraordinarily high density of predators, mostly well fed cats with nothing else to do but stalk inexperienced birds. Loose cats are probably already the reason we do not have California quail and very few fence lizards in Davis anymore; we will be even poorer without the cheerful whistling of winter sparrows.

The unfortunate high regard in which we hold cats was demonstrated in Davis in 2004. A couple of coyotes started foraging in a city greenbelt park and one of their favorite prey became cats that had been let out play with the birds. Not surprisingly, the City quickly dispatched the errant coyotes. If they had been left alone, they would have greatly reduced cat densities in the park and eventually there likely would have been an increase in nesting and migratory birds, as well as lizards and quail. This effect has been demonstrated in southern California where wild arroyos between housing tracts that have coyotes doing cat control have much more diverse faunas than those without coyotes. It is interesting to speculate how much more diverse our local parks might be if we either encouraged coyotes or required cat owners to keep their cats indoors. However, we have chosen cats over quail and lizards. Too bad cat owners have such power.

If you are too fond of your cat to euthanize it immediately, what should you do?

1. Keep it indoors, especially during fall and spring when migratory birds are most abundant. This is not as cruel you may think because cats spend so much time sleeping anyway. However, you will have to find ways to keep the animal amused and probably sacrifice some furniture and freedom from animal odors. Saving the environment involves many small sacrifices. Cats kept indoors from the time they are small kittens are typically well adjusted to their "habitat."

2. When you want to adopt a cat, obtain a kitten from someone who has an indoor cat, because hunting skills are learned in part from the mother. Keep the kitten indoors as much as possible for the first year (and thereafter).

3. Have your cat spayed or neutered.

4. If you leave an area and cannot take your cat with you, do not just turn it loose but find someone to adopt it or else have it euthanized.

5. Do not feed abandoned cats unless you plan to adopt them. The best thing to do is to capture them and turn them over to an animal shelter; otherwise you will be helping to increase the density of healthy predators on birds. The feeding of cats in public parks and on the Davis campus is particularly harmful.

EVALUATING THE AUTHOR'S ARGUMENTS:

In this viewpoint Peter Moyle is very critical of cats because they can be deadly to bird species. He suggests that cats should be euthanized (humanely put to death) rather than allowed to run wild. How should people balance their love of pets with the survival of the natural world? Did Moyle's explanation affect your opinion on the subject?

Viewpoint
5

Work Fast to Avoid Mass Extinction

James Dyke

"The ray of hope in this study is that it is possible to both reduce emissions and our impacts on biodiversity."

Scientists often look at data in different ways to form their opinions. In the following viewpoint James Dyke cites a study that suggests a lower rate of extinction than some of the other studies mentioned. This study looks at the loss of biodiversity in the last 500 years and cites the loss of total individuals rather than the number of species. Dyke then asks whether the next mass extinction can be averted. He discusses several models of how the climate might change in the future. It may be hard to both save biodiversity and stop climate change. Dyke is an Assistant Professor in Sustainability Science at the University of Southampton, England.

AS YOU READ, CONSIDER THE FOLLOWING QUESTIONS:

1. Why is biodiversity difficult to measure?

2. What percent of ancient woodland has been cut down in the United Kingdom, according to the article?

3. What areas have the worst ecological disasters, according to the author?

Humans have caused a 10% reduction in the total numbers of land-based wild animal and plants over the past 500 years, according to a major new study. We're also responsible for a 13% reduction in the number of species.

These are scary stats, but certainly more reassuring than last year's Living Planet Index report which contained the jaw-dropping statistic that over the past 40 years the total number of wild animals on Earth has been reduced by half.

So, at first glance the new research published in the journal Nature appears to downgrade the impacts humans have had on other species. However, delving deeper into the article shows large regional differences and provides yet more evidence that we are on a collision course towards mass extinction by the end of this century.

Biodiversity is by its very nature difficult to measure. In order to determine how it changes over time, repeated measurements have to be made using the same methodology in the same region. Not straightforward in remote jungles, mountains or deserts. Consequently, data sets are often very hard to come by.

Cataloguing Human Impacts

A team of scientist led by Tim Newbold at the UN Environmental Program and Microsoft Research have solved this issue by integrating very large amounts of data collected as part of the PREDICTS project. In doing so, they have created a sort of time machine. That is, they trade differences over time for differences over space.

They make the assumption that the baseline biodiversity for a particular region is the pristine undisturbed state, prior to any human impacts.

They then compare biodiversity and abundance for similar regions that have experienced progressively more human impacts such as roads, size or urban areas, density of human populations and extent of forests and plantations.

They make the assumption that a region which is heavily affected by humans would have had the same biodiversity as today's pristine example if they were able to go back far enough in time. They pick the year 1500 as a baseline with which to compare today's biodiversity. This produces the figures of 10% reduction in the abundance